SUICIDE
AND
SCANDINAVIA

A PSYCHOANALYTIC STUDY OF CULTURE AND CHARACTER

SUICIDE AND SCANDINAVIA

Herbert Hendin, M.D.

grune & stratton, inc. / new york and london / 1964

Library of Congress Catalog Card No. 64-12881

Printed in the United States of America

Contents

Preface

AFTER ten years of clinical and therapeutic research with the problem of suicide I became interested in psychoanalytic cross-cultural studies and was fortunate enough to learn something about such work directly from Dr. Abram Kardiner, a pioneer in this field.

Some combination of my interests in suicide and in cross-cultural research led me to undertake the study of the high suicide rate in Denmark. I began to see suicidal patients in Copenhagen several years ago, with little thought of going on to Sweden or Norway. Danish colleagues aroused my interest in the "Scandinavian suicide phenomenon," namely, the high suicide rates in Sweden and Denmark and the low suicide rate in Norway. After having spent a summer in Denmark, I was sufficiently impressed with what I had learned that I decided to undertake a more extensive study in Sweden.

In preparation for the work in Sweden I spent a year learning the language and reading extensively in Swedish history, economics and literature. Furthermore, I studied sources of so-called popular culture—in particular, cartoons and women's magazine stories. The work in Sweden itself likewise expanded in scope. In addition to suicidal patients (25 were studied intensively in each country), I saw more non-suicidal patients and some non-patient nurses. Psychological tests were administered to 20 of the 25 suicidal patients.

The preparations for the Norwegian study also lasted a year and were similar to those for Sweden. Learning to be fluent in Norwegian was an important part of the preliminary work. Norwegians and Swedes can generally understand each other's language; however, to establish a good relationship with Norwegian patients, it was desirable to be able to speak to them in their own language.

The study of Norwegian history, economics and literature also provided a valuable background. Norwegian sources of popular culture, i.e., folk tales, women's magazine stories and cartoons, were explored and later compared with similar material from Denmark and Sweden.

Prior to my going to Norway, Dr. Willard Gaylin and I set up a project in which non-patient American nurses were interviewed. The purpose was to determine the workability of the psychoanalytic interview technique with a group that did not have the motivation of being patients. This work, which will be reported elsewhere, was repeated with Norwegian nurses in order to obtain another yardstick with which to study the culture.

The Norwegian work was expanded in other directions. Even more non-suicidal patients were studied. Also, whereas in the Swedish study relatives of suicidal patients had been seen only occasionally, in Norway relatives of almost all of the suicidal patients were interviewed intensively.

Naturally, expansion of the project, better techniques of recording data, and simply greater experience improved each stage of the study. I am more satisfied with the Swedish than with the Danish work and more satisfied with the Norwegian than with either of the other two. Some of the Danish and Swedish data were published in psychiatric journals and elicited valuable comments from Scandinavian colleagues. These responses have been uniformly encouraging and have tended to supply more evidence of the basic observations recorded. The Norwegian material has not appeared in any form before.

HERBERT HENDIN

Acknowledgments

I WOULD LIKE FIRST to acknowledge my debt to some of those in Scandinavia whose generous help made this work possible. In Denmark the following heads of departments of psychiatry in Copenhagen gave me permission to see patients in their hospitals and outpatient clinics: Dr. Carl Clemmesen of Bispebjerg Hospital, Dr. Einar Geert-Jørgensen of Fredriksberg Hospital, Dr. Villars Lunn of Rigshospitalet, Dr. Mogens Ellermann of the Military Hospital, and Dr. Fini Schulsinger of the Kommunehospital.

Two other psychiatrists in Copenhagen were of particular help: Dr. Grethe Pærregaard of Bispebjerg Hospital, who has been working with the problem of suicide, and Dr. Gudrun Brun, child psychiatrist at Bispebjerg.

Professor Lise Østergaard, formerly psychologist at Rigshospitalet, and Miss Kirsten Rudfeld of the Sociological Institute of the University of Copenhagen (who has also worked with the problem of suicide) both discussed aspects of my work with me. Miss Karen Dreyer, of the statistical section of the National Health Service, has studied both Danish and international suicide statistics and was always generous with her time both in talking to me and in answering questions by letter.

In Sweden, Professor Snorre Wohlfahrt, formerly head of the psychiatric division at Södersjukhuset, not only permitted me to work freely at Södersjukhuset but also aided and advised me whenever necessary. Dr. Ruth Ettlinger, assistant director of the psychiatric division at Södersjukhuset and long interested in the problem of suicide, helped me personally and professionally in a hundred ways in connection with this work. The same is also true of Dr. Karin Hellgren, child psychiatrist (now at Rådgivningsbyrån in Huddinge), with whom I exchanged many ideas. Miss Marianne Lundgren, psychologist at Södersjukhuset, did the psychological testing and gave unsparingly of her time in discussing the cases. Dr. Johan Cullberg and the late

Dr. Lennart Djurfeldt, both then at Södersjukhuset, generously helped me with practical details concerning the work.

Docent Curt Åmark, division head of psychiatry at Långbro Hospital, allowed me to interview the patients and nurses at Långbro. Also helpful to me at Långbro were Dr. Brita Åstrand of the psychiatric staff and Dr. Olena Sennton, psychologist at the hospital.

Mrs. Carin Colliander, head of the Family Guidance Clinic in Stockholm, discussed with me some of the family problems seen at the clinic, and Mr. Sten Kruse of the Swedish Central Bureau of Statistics helped me with the statistical material concerning suicide in Sweden.

The following Swedish psychoanalysts discussed with me aspects of the Swedish work in which they were particularly interested: Dr. Annastina Rilton, Dr. Lajos Székely, Dr. Edith Székely, Dr. Gösta Harding, director of the Erica Foundation, and Dr. Kjell Öhrberg, head of Mentalvårdsbyrån.

In Norway, Professor Ørnulv Ødegård of Gaustad Hospital in Oslo advised me with regard to the project and gave me permission to see patients transferred to Gaustad from Ullevål Hospital during this study.

The following doctors at Ullevål Hospital in Oslo were most directly involved in permitting me to work at the hospital: Dr. Per Anchersen, head of the Psychiatric Division for Men; Dr. Herluf Thomstad, head of the Psychiatric Division for Women; Dr. Irmelin Christensen (now retired), head of the psychiatric ward, run in cooperation with the Oslo police; Professor Einar Blegen, head of the 7th Medical Division; Professor Anton Jervell, head of the 8th Medical Division; Professor Knut Aas, head of the 9th Medical Division; Professor Carl Semb, head of the 3rd Surgical Division.

Mrs. Annie Von der Lippe and Mrs. Barbro Selnes, both of Ullevål Hospital, did the psychological testing in Norway.

Mrs. Ellen Blix of the Norwegian Central Bureau of Statistics helped me with statistical data on suicide in Norway and in Scandinavia as a whole.

Dr. Hjalmar Wergeland, head of the Department of Child Psychiatry at Rikshospitalet in Oslo, gave me helpful advice concerning this work. Docent Åse Gruda Skard, child psychologist of the Oslo University Institute of Psychology, also discussed certain aspects of the work with me.

Dr. Per Sundby of the Ullevål Psychiatric Division for Men and Dr. Hilchen Sundby of the Department of Child Psychiatry at Rikshospitalet were both most helpful in discussing my work with me and in advising and encouraging me with regard to it.

Finally, I would like to thank all the nurses and residents who helped me daily in my work and all the Scandinavian friends who made living and working in the three countries a pleasure.

In this country too I received extremely valuable help and would like to thank the persons and organizations indicated below.

The American-Scandinavian Foundation (Peter Strong, Executive Director) made me an Honorary Fellow and also sponsored my application for a grant to the National Institute of Mental Health.

Mrs. Margareta Hunt, then of the American-Scandinavian Foundation, helped me learn Swedish and assisted in matters ranging from Swedish literature to organization of the project in Sweden.

The National Institute of Mental Health of the U.S. Public Health Service supported the Norwegian work (Research Grant MH 07207-01) and made completion of this project possible.

Directly responsible for giving me permission to see suicidal patients at Bellevue Hospital were Dr. S. Bernard Wortis, Professor of Psychiatry and Chairman of the Departments of Psychiatry and Neurology, New York University; Dr. Morris Herman, Professor of Psychiatry, New York University; Dr. Lewis Sharp, former Director of the Psychiatric Division of Bellevue Hospital; Dr. Arthur Zitrin, Director of the Psychiatric Division of Bellevue Hospital.

Dr. Lawrence Kolb, Professor of Psychiatry and Chairman of the Department of Psychiatry, Columbia University, gave me permission to see suicidal patients at The Psychiatric Institute.

Dr. Joseph Cotton, Chief of Psychiatry at St. Luke's Hospital, gave me permission to see suicidal patients at St. Luke's Hospital.

Dr. George S. Goldman, Director of the Columbia University Psychoanalytic Clinic, encouraged me in this work and limited my duties at the Clinic so as to give me more time for the project.

The Adele Levy Research Fund of the Psychoanalytic Clinic gave me a grant that helped support the Swedish part of this work.

Dr. Abram Kardiner, Dr. Willard Gaylin and Dr. Ruth Easser, all of the Columbia University Psychoanalytic Clinic, read the manuscript and made valuable suggestions for improving it.

Dr. Franz Kallmann, Chairman of the Editorial Committee of the Columbia University Department of Psychiatry, read and approved the manuscript. I am especially grateful to him for the unlimited time he gave to editing the text.

Professor John C. Nelson of Columbia University gave invaluable help in the final editing of the manuscript.

The Psychiatric Quarterly, the McGraw-Hill Co., Williams & Wilkins Co., publisher of the Journal of Nervous and Mental Disease, and the Columbia University Forum gave permission to use material from previously published articles.

Miss Herbjørg Lund worked as secretary for the project and typed the final manuscript.

My mother carefully read and corrected the manuscript and my father made helpful suggestions.

Miss Reidun Ytreeide served as my assistant both in this country and in Norway. She helped me learn Norwegian and assisted in the analysis of hundreds of magazine stories and cartoons from all three Scandinavian countries. She also gave constant help and encouragement in the writing of this book.

CHAPTER I

The Problem

WHAT motivates a Dane to suicide? Are his reasons different from those of a Norwegian or Swede? What light do his reasons throw on the particular pressures and tensions within his country? What is the explanation of the "Scandinavian suicide phenomenon," i.e., the strikingly high suicide rates in Denmark and Sweden and the remarkably low suicide rate in Norway?

Such questions lead to a consideration of what has been called national character. Most of the formal study of national character[1] has come from anthropologists and sociologists who have gradually realized that to describe social institutions is one thing, while to study their effect on individual character is quite another. For this latter task a sensitive psychological instrument is required. Many social scientists have been hopeful that psychoanalysis will fill this need.

In his pioneering work with primitive societies Kardiner[2] demonstrated the value of psychoanalysis in establishing the role played by variations in social institutions in shaping the kind of individual produced by a given society. However, the major focus of his work was on the vast differences among primitive cultures and between them and ourselves rather than on the finer integrative differences seen among modern societies.

In the course of this present study, through the use of a psychoanalytic approach to interviewing, essential character differences were found among Danes, Swedes and Norwegians. I hope to show that these differences can be determined and their origins traced even in three such related modern cultures.

The approach to interviewing is crucial. A question-and-answer technique, even when conducted by a psychiatrically trained observer and even when the subject does not consciously wish to conceal information, is of limited value. It usually

---

[1] This and subsequent numbered notes, primarily references, will be found on pp. 141 to 147.

reflects what the subject wants to feel, thinks he feels or thinks he is expected to feel. An interview technique relying on free associations, unconscious reactions, dreams and fantasies is superior because the subject reveals his inner feelings often without awareness or intention on his part.

For example, in his sociological survey of Norway, Rodnick[3] accepts at face value statements by Norwegian women that the woman plays a completely submissive role in Norwegian marriages. However, if Norwegian women expressing this opinion begin to talk freely about their own lives, one discovers that they actually consider themselves stronger than their husbands, that their mothers dominated their fathers, and that the woman is the effective figure in most of their friends' marriages. They will often dream of their men as babies or children. If pressed about this contradiction they will usually admit that "women are stronger than men, but a man must be allowed to think he is stronger."

What people think they should feel is indicative of certain social values present in the culture. Their inner feelings and attitudes may be quite different. When asked if she were a good nurse, not one of 12 Norwegian nurses would say yes. "I'm average" or "my superiors think I'm all right" was the usual reply. Of 12 American nurses, all but one stated that they considered themselves good nurses. However, rather than indicating less self-confidence on the part of the Norwegian nurses, the Norwegian replies reflected a different cultural attitude: to say you were good was something you simply did not do. The American girls reflected the attitude that if you did not project a feeling of belief in your own competence, certainly no one else would believe in it.

Social attitudes of this kind are not difficult to ascertain, although they tell us relatively little. Unconscious psychodynamic attitudes, such as that of dealing with men by visualizing them as children, can only be determined by free associations, dreams, etc. "Psychosocial character" is probably a more accurate term than "national character" as a shorthand description of this combination of conscious and unconscious attitudes. In the present study interest is centered on the predominant social attitudes and psychodynamic constellations, rather than on individual

idiosyncrasies. Emphasis will naturally fall on those aspects of
psychosocial character that distinguish Norway, Denmark and
Sweden, particularly when such constellations have a bearing
on the problem of suicide.

In general the suicidal patient proved to be a different entity
in each of the three Scandinavian countries. These differences
reflected vastly different cultural attitudes and psychological
problems. One premise implicit in such work is that both
suicidal patients and non-suicidal patients reflect pressures that
are exerted on everyone in the society whether he succumbs to
them or not. It was partly to test this premise and partly to have
another source of information about each culture that I began
interviewing non-patients in Scandinavia, and worked with Dr.
Willard Gaylin in this country, in developing a method for applying psychoanalytic interviewing techniques to the study of non-
patients.[4] Differences observed among the non-patients in Scandinavia correlated well with differences between suicidal patients
and non-suicidal patients in the three countries. As a psychosocial
barometer, the suicidal patients have one advantage over non-
suicidal patients. Since they are most often emergency admissions to the hospital, patients with the economic means to otherwise choose private facilities for treatment become part of the
public hospital population. Thus the suicidal patients present
a much broader spectrum of occupational, economic and social
class than do other groups of patients admitted to a public
hospital.

Another premise implicit in this work is that one can draw
significant conclusions regarding the people in the three Scandinavian countries from a psychodynamic study of altogether
less than 200 individuals. I can best clarify this statement by a
comparison with New York City, which with its immediate en-
virons has a population roughly equivalent to that of the three
Scandinavian countries.

If a psychoanalytically trained observer, with a frame of reference extending to the society as well as the individual, sees in
New York City only five Italian, five Irish and five Jewish patients,
he can already begin to construct a picture of the differences in
the family patterns, character and attitudes seen in people from
these three backgrounds. By the time he sees a dozen of each

group, distinctions will have become quite clear. The observer must take into consideration not only how long the Jewish, Italian or Irish family has been in the United States but also from what part of Italy, Ireland or Europe they came. However, if he is concerned only with those features which characterize each group as a whole, a total of 50 subjects will probably suffice. More important than the number of people, is the method used for observing them.

                    ✿   ✿   ✿

Danish and Swedish suicide rates have been among the world's highest, averaging close to 20 suicides per 100,000 population.[5] These rates are equalled by those in Japan, Switzerland, Germany and Austria; however, with the exception of the Japanese rate, the Swedish and Danish rates are the most publicized.

Much of the attention which the high Danish and Swedish suicide rates have received is a consequence of the social welfare measures applied in the two countries. Both inside and outside Sweden and Denmark, opponents of economic planning and social welfare measures have attempted to explain the suicide rate as a consequence of character defects produced by these measures. But the Danish suicide rate has been higher than those of most other European countries for the last hundred years.[6] The Swedish suicide rate has climbed since the turn of the century, and a better case could be made for relating this rise to Sweden's late but fast developing industrial capitalism than can be made for relating it to the relatively recent social welfare measures.

Inasmuch as Sweden has been successful in dealing with most of the economic problems that plague the rest of the world, it has been felt that her people have "no right" to a high suicide rate. However, it has long been known that countries with much poverty have low suicide rates. One can hardly suggest planned poverty as a cure for suicide. Economic difficulties and problems of survival can suppress psychological conflicts. Only as countries begin to solve the problems of survival are they in a position even to become aware of the psychosocial tensions and conflicts within the culture.

Suicide is but one barometer of social tension; crime, alcoholism and neurosis are equally barometers, and one such index
cannot be consulted without reference to all the others. For example, while the suicide rates for Sweden and Denmark are twice
that of the United States, the homicide rate in the United States
is ten times that of the Scandinavian countries.

Throughout this century the Danish and Swedish suicide rates
have averaged almost three times the strikingly low Norwegian
rate—currently 7.5 suicides per 100,000 population. However, if
certain social institutions in Sweden and Denmark play a significant role in their high suicide rates, a comparative study of
these same institutions in Norway is in order.

Not only the welfare state, but also bad weather and good statistical bureaus have been blamed for the high Danish and
Swedish suicide rates. But Norway has equally advanced social
welfare measures, equally bad weather and a statistical bureau
of comparable accuracy to those of Sweden and Denmark. When
the statistical question was discussed in detail with the person in
charge of suicide statistics in each of the three countries, we
could find no evidence that would support a statistical explanation.[7]

The ratio of about 3 to 1 of suicide rates for Sweden and Denmark as compared with Norway holds true if one breaks down
the figures and makes cross-cultural statistical comparisons of
urban or rural areas in the respective countries; if one separates
the sexes and compares Swedish and Danish men with Norwegian
men or Swedish and Danish women with Norwegian women, the
same marked preponderance of Swedish and Danish suicides
over Norwegian suicides remains evident. The situation is the
same when the population is broken up into different age groups
or divided on the basis of marital status. The absolute figures, of
course, will vary so that, as with modern Western countries in
general, the old have higher rates than the young, men higher
rates than women, and the divorced higher rates than the married.
However, the relative rates or ratios obtained by comparing each
of these social and statistical categories with the corresponding
group in Norway fall in a general range of between 2.5 and 5
to 1.

Of course, it is easier for suicides to remain unreported in the
rural areas of all countries, and countries differ in the proportions

of their rural populations. For this reason it was useful to compare the suicide rates for such major cities as Copenhagen, Stockholm and Oslo. An additional advantage of this procedure is that in major cities the routine for dealing with deaths due to suicide tends to be more uniform. The suicide rates for all these cities are higher than for their respective countries (for many reasons apart from statistical accuracy), but the information yielded by comparing them correlates well with that revealed by a comparison of the three countries. The Stockholm and Copenhagen suicide rates are about three times the Oslo rate, just as the rates for Sweden and Denmark are about three times the rate for Norway.

There is still the possibility that even in large cities only the Danish and Swedish doctors tend to report "honestly" because of less social pressure to conceal suicide. Over the past few years I have been informally questioning doctors in the three countries concerning their practice in this regard. While little can as yet be said as to the practice in the rural districts, there is no reason to believe that significant differences exist among the doctors in the major cities.

A similar question is often raised in relation to the Catholic countries which, except for Austria, have very low suicide rates. It is claimed that with more shame attached to suicide in these countries, there is a stronger tendency toward concealment of suicide even among the doctors than there would be in Scandinavia. It is evident, however, that such concealment might affect but will not significantly alter the comparative suicide rates. In a country with a strong religious or moral prohibition against suicide there is likely to be more concealment of suicide, but more importantly there is also likely to be less suicide. Thus the doctor's attitude toward suicide is largely a reflection of the society's attitude toward suicide, and the society's attitude toward suicide has an important bearing on the suicidal rate.

❋   ❋   ❋

The American psychiatrist or psychoanalyst, whose interest in suicide is primarily clinical, may wonder what he can learn from the case histories of patients who are mainly Norwegians, Danes and Swedes (except for those in Chapter 3). However, the opportunity to study suicidal patients in various cultures provides a new perspective for understanding the psychodynamics of suicide, thus yielding answers to many puzzling clinical and psychodynamic problems concerning suicide. Hence, in addition to the twin objectives of trying to understand the "Scandinavian suicide phenomenon" and attempting to define the psychosocial character within all three Scandinavian countries, this study has an equally important third goal. The aim has been to make use of this material so as to broaden our understanding of the individual suicide and of its significance within different cultures.

CHAPTER II

Durkheim and Freud:
Background of the Problem

THE FIRST MAJOR CONTRIBUTION to the study of the problem of suicide was made at the end of the last century by the French sociologist, Emile Durkheim.[1] Many of his basic concepts are still actively in use, although sociologists have refined and extended his original contribution.

Durkheim analyzed the European suicide figures mainly of the last half of the nineteenth century. He focused attention on some of the characteristic statistical patterns noted in the last chapter and on others as well. Suicide was more common in cities than in rural districts; there was more suicide among the single and the divorced than among the married; more among the married who were childless than in parents; it was seen more frequently in men than in women; more frequently among the wealthy than the poor, and more frequently among Protestants than Catholics. These general statistical findings have held true in both Europe and the United States in our century as well.[2]

In an attempt to explain these statistical facts, Durkheim divided suicides into three social categories (egoistic, altruistic and anomic) which may be briefly described here. Egoistic suicide comprised individuals who were assumed not to have been strongly integrated into any social group regardless of whether that group was a family, a religion or a community. Family integration or the lack of it could be used to explain why the unmarried were more vulnerable to suicide than the married and why couples with children were the best protected group of all. Rural communities had more social integration than urban areas and thus less suicide. Protestantism was a less cohesive religion than Catholicism, and Protestants thus had a higher suicide rate than Catholics.

Altruistic suicide described the group whose proneness to suicide stemmed from exactly the opposite factor, i.e., their excessive integration into a group, with suicide being the outgrowth of this integration. Durkheim had in mind the kind of suicide that in special situations could be expected of certain classes in Japanese society, and also the kind of integration into a military group that could at times require an individual to sacrifice his life.

Anomic suicide occurs when there is a disturbance in the balance of the individual's integration with society which leaves him without his customary norms of behavior. Anomie could explain the greater incidence of suicide among the divorced as compared to the married and the greater vulnerability of those who had undergone drastic changes in their economic situation. As a corollary of anomie, greater vulnerability to suicide was seen to exist among those in the society who had wealth or status and thus had more that they could potentially lose. It is among the wealthy who have had money and lost it, and not among the poorer classes, that one sees an increase in suicide during periods of economic depression. Negroes in the United States have a much lower suicide rate than whites, and sociologists could now explain this as due to the Negro's lower status and consequently lesser vulnerability to anomic suicide.

Increases in anomic and egoistic suicide were felt by Durkheim to be responsible for the rising suicide rates of Europe. The rise originated in a "pathological state just now accompanying the march of civilization without being its necessary condition." With industrial and scientific development neither the family, the state nor the church were the forces for social integration they had once been, and nothing had been found to replace them.

In essence Durkheim's contribution was the introduction of the social dimension into the problem of suicide. He showed that suicide, like crime, neurosis and alcoholism is a factor that measures social pressure and tension. The extremely high rate seen in West Berlin in the post-war period is perhaps the most dramatic manifestation of this principle.

Durkheim's social categories were used to explain the variations in the rate of suicide from country to country. The Catholic countries had low suicide rates in line with Durkheim's observations on the influence of Catholicism. Low rates were seen in impoverished countries like Spain and Ireland, although here a combination of being both poor and Catholic may have been at work. Such wide application of Durkheim's work was bound to highlight some of its weaknesses. No satisfactory explanation was given by Durkheim or his followers for Austria, a Catholic country with one of the world's highest suicide rates. No adequate explanation for the Scandinavian phenomenon of the strikingly high Danish and Swedish suicide rates as compared with the low rate in Norway could be found in Durkheim's categories.

Durkheim was neither oriented toward nor interested in the psychology of the individual suicide. This attitude was but an extension of his general feeling that "social facts must be studied as things, as realities external to the individual" and that therefore the psychology of the individual had little relevance for sociology. Since we are still busy resolving the problem of effectively integrating psychological and sociological data, it would not be fair to criticize Durkheim too severely for not tackling this problem. In the light of current knowledge it is easy to see how the omission of the individual dimension limited the contribution that Durkheim could make in his own field of interest. The ways in which different social and cultural institutions are integrated by the individual and affect his development, personality and character are not only important to psychology, but since the individual is the ultimate measure of the impact of social pressures, ignoring him makes the sociologist's study of social pressures something of guess work.

The first important psychological insight into suicide came from Freud. Freud did not deal directly with the problem of suicide and described only one patient who actually made a suicide attempt.[3] What he did see, however, and in good number, were depressed patients. In "Mourning and Melancholia" (1916) Freud stated that the self-hatred seen in depression originated in anger toward a love object that the individual turned back on himself.[4] He regarded suicide as the ultimate form of this phenomenon and doubted that there would be a suicide without the earlier repressed desire to kill someone else. This concept of suicide as a kind of inverted murder was extremely important, although, unfortunately, it became overworked by some in an effort to explain all suicide.

Freud's observations on depression were made long before he came to the conclusion that anger or aggression could be non-erotic in origin. At the time of the writing of "Mourning and Melancholia" all aggression had to have, in Freud's view, a sexual origin. Hence this article is filled with a complex discussion of what amounts to retroflexed anger. Ten years later Freud expressed surprise at his having overlooked "the universality of non-erotic aggression."[5] Since he never rewrote his earlier report, the extraneous libidinal explanations for the existence of anger remained unaltered. However, this fact should not lead one to overlook the basic psychological truth contained in the 1916 paper; namely, that anger can become self-directed, can lead to depression, and can be a motivating force in suicide.

Freud's preference for instinctual explanations had led him to see aggression as the manifestation of a death instinct (1920).[6] The death instinct violated too many basic observations of biologists and psychologists for it ever to be accepted by them or by more than a small minority of psychoanalysts. "Instinct psychology" soon lost much of its influence in the field of psychology although it has held on longer in psychoanalysis. By 1922 John Dewey[7] had already given his analysis of the misconceptions that arose from taking a phenomenon and elevating it to a cause by attributing it to an instinct. Zilboorg[8] probably spoke for a majority of psychoanalysts* when he wrote in 1937 that "to say the death instinct gains the upper hand over the life instinct is merely an elaborate way of saying that man does die or kill himself."

While Durkheim minimized the individual dimension, Freud showed a similar disregard for the social dimension. Instincts know no societal boundaries, and Freud's instinctual frame of reference did not lead him to a concern with the psychological impact of the social institutions of particular cultures nor with such psychosocial questions as to why suicide was very high in one country and very low in another. Nor would his instinctual frame of reference have enabled him to resolve adequately such

---

* Menninger[9] is the major figure working with suicide who has continued to accept and utilize the concept of a death instinct. However, he was careful to separate the hypothesis of the death instinct from the clinical phenomena for which he had evidence. Hence his demonstration of the various manifestations of self-destructiveness, whether acutely in suicide or chronically in alcoholism, antisocial behavior, etc., remains of value despite his acceptance of the death instinct as a basic premise.

questions, even if they had arisen. The marked variation in the suicide rates from country to country had helped Durkheim realize that "social facts" were a function of social institutions which in turn were a function of a particular society or culture. Biologically speaking, the differences between Englishmen and Germans or Norwegians and Swedes are not very important, and Freud assumed he was dealing with psychological evolution much as Darwin had dealt with biological evolution. Being understandably under the influence of the evolutionary anthropology of his day, Freud saw the psychological life of primitive man as "a well preserved early stage of our own development."[10] This approach made study of the culture as a unit unnecessary, and Freud had little interest in the comparative anthropology that developed during his lifetime.

More important was his influence. As late as 1936 Zilboorg was certain that investigation would show primitive man to have a much higher suicide rate than modern man.[11] Investigation showed rather that primitive cultures also had marked variations in suicide rates and that there were cultures where it was unknown. In any case, separate study of each culture, its people and psychosocial institutions, is required for any deeper understanding of the frequency with which suicide is used in a society as an expression of personal dissatisfaction and unhappiness.

A psychosocial phenomenon such as suicide must be studied psychologically and socially. Neither approach by itself is adequate. A sociological approach provides no way of evaluating the relative impact of different social pressures and tends to be blind or at best weak in seeing how social forces are integrated by the individual personality. On the other hand, psychiatric thinking that starts with the individual and never leaves the individual can be equally blind in understanding the specific psychosocial attitudes within the culture and the role they play in shaping the individual personality. It was no accident that the great contributions of early psychoanalysis were to the study of the individual and not to the study of the society. At the Columbia University Psychoanalytic Clinic, with which the author is affiliated, an attempt has been made to develop a psychoanalytic frame of reference that is workable in studying both the individual and the culture in which he lives.

CHAPTER III

The Psychodynamics of Suicide

INSIGHT INTO THE PSYCHODYNAMICS of suicide is a prerequisite for an understanding of suicide as it is seen in the Scandinavian countries. As was indicated in the preceding chapter, modern concepts of the psychodynamics of suicide began with Freud's idea that suicide stemmed from anger toward a love object that had become self-directed and was thus a kind of inverted homicide. It should also be recalled that Freud's theory was the outgrowth of his work with depression.

Current views of depression have been revised over the years. The significance of both dependency and expiation in depression was stressed by Sandor Rado.[1] The idea that retroflexed anger and self-punishment can have atonement or expiation as goals—with the depressed individual hoping to win back love and affection—does not appear in "Mourning and Melancholia" and was primarily Rado's contribution. Just as retroflexed anger can at times be the motivating force in suicidal patients, so can suicide be an act of expiation.

Despite the help that the knowledge of the psychology of depression gives to the understanding of suicide, it is by no means the whole picture. A great number of suicidal patients do not manifest the clinical features or classic psychodynamics associated with depression. Especially important is the fact that many depressed patients are not suicidal. This observation alone serves to demonstrate that the psychodynamic aspects of depression are not sufficient to explain suicide. In other words, the study of depressed patients cannot be used as a substitute for the direct examination of suicidal patients. In such investigations many suicidal patients appear to view their death as an internalized murder, while the suicide attempts of others are explained as acts of expiation. In addition, there is a broad range of different attitudes toward death and other meanings of the act of suicide.

How to Study the Problem

This study of the problem of suicide began at Bellevue Hospital in New York City with interviews of 100 consecutive admissions of attempted suicide. These patients were seen as often as seemed necessary for obtaining a full psychodynamic picture of each case. Later on, patients who had made suicide attempts were taken into therapy with the emphasis being placed on collecting a diversified series of suicidal motivations and situations. As many as 15 suicidal patients were in therapy with me at one period during this investigation. In addition, my current work at St. Luke's Hospital has been extended by use of hypnosis in an attempt to learn the psychodynamics of individual patients and their motivations for suicide. In all these approaches, however, as well as in cross-cultural work with suicidal patients in Scandinavia, the patients seen have attempted to commit suicide and, obviously, survived. Therefore the question is often raised whether those who attempted suicide and survived are comparable in terms of personality and motivation to those who actually died. This question bears on any evaluation of the psychodynamics of suicide.

Some years ago it proved helpful to rate or evaluate suicidal patients on a scale of one to three with regard to their suicidal intent (1—the patient with minimal intent; 2—moderate intent; 3—maximal suicidal intent).[2] The following two cases illustrate types of patients in the maximal intent group: one was a girl who jumped under a subway train and survived, although two cars passed over her. Her survival was possible on this particular subway since there was sufficient room between the wheels and under the train. However, these details were not known by the girl at that time. A second patient entered into a suicide pact with his homosexual partner. They made their attempt in a hotel room on a Saturday night so that they would not be discovered by the chambermaid until Monday morning. Both took 50 barbiturates of 1/10th gram strength. When found and admitted to the hospital on Monday, they were comatose and remained so for several days. The initial opinion of the hospital staff was that neither would survive. As it turned out, one died and the other lived. The one who lived was placed in the group of maximal intent patients.

It seems reasonable to include the girl who jumped under the train as well as the homosexual man in the maximal intent group and to assume that in working with them one encounters a situation as close as is necessary to that resulting in actual suicide. When suicidal patients are divided into intent groups, the group with maximal intent has an age and sex distribution statistically comparable to that of actual suicide. It is quite different from the total group of all attempted suicides.[2]

Farberow and Schneidman,[3] in a study of actual suicides, found that 62 per cent of them had histories of previous attempts. When they added to this percentage the patients who had made suicidal threats, the figure rose to 75 per cent, seemingly conflicting with the data of Stengel[4] and Ettlinger.[5] The latter followed patients who had attempted suicide and survived and established that 10 per cent of them eventually did kill themselves. The three studies taken together make it appear likely that the attempted suicide group is a large and heterogeneous group which in a sense "contains" the eventual suicide group. In any case the studies highlight both the research value and the clinical necessity of the careful evaluation of attempted suicide.

A great deal about suicide can also be learned from the study of patients in the lower intent groups. When, for example, suicide is an act of self-punishment, for one patient only death will be sufficient atonement, while for another the self-damage done in a suicide attempt may suffice. The study of both types, however, throws light on the psychology of self-punishment and its relation to suicide.

Then too, just as patients whose intent to die is strong may by accident survive, one sees patients with low suicidal intent whose attempt somehow results in their death. A young Puerto Rican boy picked up and swallowed some insecticide in front of his girl friend during a lovers' quarrel. He wished to coerce her into both sympathy and affection, typifying scores of such cases seen at Bellevue. His suicidal intent was minimal and he fully expected to survive. Unwittingly, however, he had taken an insecticide then on the market which contained arsenic. His initial dismay and subsequent despair in the hospital on seeing that he would not recover were quite genuine. He eventually died due to liver and kidney poisoning. His case and many similar ones indicate that even patients with low suicidal intent represent a definite part of the suicide problem.

The distinction between a patient who is very serious about suicide and one who is not serious at all is not particularly difficult; however, the situation is more complicated with patients who are in the intermediate group. Patients who survived taking as many as 25 sleeping pills may say that they only wished to sleep. Nevertheless, they may admit having had the thought that it might have been pleasant never to wake up. Sometimes they appear unsure as to whether they wanted to die. Undoubtedly most suicidal patients have mixed feelings about the wish to die. Menninger in particular has pointed to some of the variations seen in patients' conscious and unconscious wishes with regard to dying.[6] In Anna Karenina, Tolstoy describes the heroine's last feelings and sensations after jumping in front of a train. She feels that she may have made a mistake and struggles unsuccessfully to get up before the train hits her. Tolstoy's sensitive intuition in this regard seems very much borne out by what is learned from actual suicidal patients. It is possible that if a man jumping from a tall building could be interviewed while still in the air three floors down from the top, his feelings about dying might be different from what they had been a few seconds earlier. A recently interviewed patient said she had wished to change her mind right before jumping from a building; however, since she had committed herself in a letter to this action, she was unable to back out.

Hypnosis can be useful in evaluating a patient's suicidal intent as well as his motives. It is of obvious use in reconstructing and recovering amnesias connected with suicide attempts. Patients who were under the influence of alcohol at the time and are vague as to the details of the attempt can often recall them under hypnosis. Similarly, one patient who shot himself and survived was amnestic for all the events that took place shortly before pulling the trigger of the shotgun. Under hypnosis his thoughts and feelings during that period as well as the details of his attempt were recovered.

The most important use of hypnosis as a research tool in studying suicide is in another area. It will be shown in greater detail in the subsequent section on the psychodynamics of suicide that the dreams of these patients immediately before or after their suicide attempt often reveal their motives for wishing to die. Hence they are of great value in getting a psychodynamic picture of the patient. When patients are interviewed soon after their attempts, the dynamics are close to consciousness and are apt to be revealed in their dreams. When months have elapsed, these dynamics are likely to have been so repressed that a patient may have to be seen in therapy for a long time before the material becomes similiarly accessible. Thus it is generally advisable to see patients within the first few days after their attempted suicide. When patients are unable to remember dreams during the period of their suicide attempts, hypnosis can be of value. I have asked hypnotized patients to go back in their thoughts to the time of their attempt and to the mood of that time. The suggestion was then made that while under hypnosis they would have a dream similar to the one which they might have had before their suicide attempt. It was also suggested that this dream would throw some light on their reasons for wanting to kill themselves. Although such a technique proved productive with only about a third of suicidal patients, when successful it yielded invaluable material from the research standpoint. In discussing the psychodynamics of suicide some of this material will be considered.

The Psychodynamics of Suicide

Since the methodological details and particular circumstances of a suicide attempt usually provide us with the first important clue as to the psychodynamics of a particular patient, they must be carefully established. With the suicide attempt often representing a kind of psychological drama, the very way in which it is made is apt to be revealing. One woman jumped from a window with a picture of her son in her brassiere and a message on the back of the picture saying, "Timmy knows I love him." Years before, at the time of her divorce, this woman had given away her young son to his paternal grandparents, who actually raised him. While she still saw him up to the time of the attempt, she was tortured by her difficulties in love relationships and especially by her inability to love her son. The picture and its message amounted to an attempt to deny the true state of affairs. Yet they furnished the first insight into her desire to end her life.

In another case, an elderly man who wanted to kill himself with barbiturates arranged his attempt in such a way that he could be found by his son before death. The man had been separated from his wife for a year after 25 years of marriage; and it first appeared that the severed relationship with his wife was the crucial motivational factor. After three days in the hospital, however, he reported a dream in which his son fed him poison. Only then it became possible to recognize the patient's relationship with his son as the major determinant in this case.

In many instances the choice of method used in a suicide may reveal a good deal about the organization and integration of the personality involved. Disorganized or multiple suicidal methods or those carried out in a chaotic manner and lasting several days are usually chosen by disorganized, schizoid patients.

Freud[7] had written in 1915 that the "unconscious does not believe in its own death." Some 20 years later Zilboorg elaborated on this statement to stress the importance of unconscious fantasies of immortality, particularly for suicidal patients.[8] It may seem surprising that since then there has not been more systematic investigation of the attitudes and fantasies of suicidal patients toward death, dying and afterlife. This can partly be attributed to the anxiety and inhibition of psychiatrists in relation to suicidal patients.[9] A reflection of this attitude can be seen among the residents of psychiatric wards who will ask a patient after ten minutes' acquaintance if he has had homosexual experiences or what he does with regard to masturbation. However, they will probably fail to ask a suicidal patient about his attitudes toward death, about the presumed events after death, about his thoughts after he turned on the gas and about possible dreams during his state of unconsciousness. These four questions can elicit valuable material bearing on the understanding of suicidal patients and their motivation. The answers to them make clear that what a suicidal patient wishes to escape from in life tells us only part of his story. His attitudes toward death, dying and afterlife must be known in order to understand fully his motivations for suicide.

The following case illustrations pertain to patients seen by me either in New York City at Bellevue Hospital, the New York State Psychiatric Institute or at St. Luke's Hospital, or in one of the three Scandinavian countries.[10] They illustrate some of the psychodynamic constellations with regard to death and suicide that have been observed in suicidal patients.

Death as retaliatory abandonment: An 18 year old homosexual college boy who had been failing in school was seen following a serious suicide attempt with 60 barbiturates which he barely survived. During a hypnotic interview it was suggested to the patient that he would have a dream such as he might have had during the night of his suicidal attempt. His dream was a simple one. He was working for the United Nations where he had an office comprising the entire first floor of the UN building. He was interviewing one of his friends who was applying for a position, and was reviewing his qualifications. Finally he told his friend that he did not qualify for the job.

During his waking associations to the dream he revealed his preoccupation with this friend on whom he had had a "crush," although he had never mentioned to the boy his sexual interest in him. Apparently the friend became alarmed at the intensity of the patient's feelings and was determined to break away from the relationship. Several months prior to the suicide attempt he had stopped seeing the patient.

What does the patient accomplish in the dream and by his suicide attempt? He gains an illusory control over the situation in which he was rejected. In the dream, if there has to be a rejection, he is going to do it; by committing suicide, he is the one who leaves and rejects. The concept of death as an act of leaving, i.e., an abandonment, is known to derive from childhood. Children's reactions to death frequently imply either that a violent act was inflicted on the dead person or that he "left" voluntarily. Children who lose or are separated from their mothers invariably react as though the mothers had chosen to leave them. The continuation of this psychological equation is seen in adult patients with extreme fears of dying, which are traceable to the most primitive abandonment fears of childhood.

That the last patient also experienced *a feeling of omnipotent mastery through death* is strongly suggested by the important UN position and large office in his dream. Suicide attempts and the possibility of suicide seem to give a person an illusory feeling of mastery over a situation through the control over life and death.

Another patient, a chemistry major in college, had struggled through school with a cyanide capsule in his desk, consoling himself with the thought that if he could not manage his work, he could always take the cyanide. On graduation he threw it out and never made a suicide attempt. On the other hand, a female patient who eventually did make a serious suicide attempt had previously kept a toy pistol in her drawer and had comforted herself through an unhappy love affair with the fantasy that if things got too bad she could always kill herself.

Death as retroflexed murder: A 44 year old woman made a suicide attempt with sleeping pills about a year after the breakup of her marriage. Her husband had been unfaithful during the 20 years of their marriage while she had alternately doubted these affairs or had reassured herself by saying that they were unimportant to him. However, his last affair lasted almost two years. Finally she precipitated a crisis by barging in on him in the other woman's apartment. He was furious and openly moved in with this woman. About six months later she had a rather unsatisfactory love affair with a younger man. Immediately following her suicide attempt she stated that both her children and her husband would be better off without her. Especially the children, a boy 19 and a girl of 15, she said, needed a new home.

In an attempt ten days earlier she had gone out to a lake with the intention of drowning herself but changed her mind. She came home and took 15 sleeping pills instead, waking up by herself a day and a half later. The next time she took twice that dose. While under the influence of the first pills she had the following dream. She saw a cap belonging to her husband's father floating on the sea and realized that he had drowned. Her husband's father had been a sea captain and closely resembled her husband, being extremely domineering, critical and difficult to get along with. At first she saw the dream in terms of her own martyred role, but eventually she related it to her desire to strike back at her husband. She spoke vindictively of the problem which the children would cause him after her death. It soon became evident that her suicide attempt stemmed from her anger at her husband and was an indirect attempt at revenge. She was ineffective in handling both her anger and self-assertion and she could not even fight for her children. Her situation was like the classic one described by Freud in which suicide represents an inverted homicide.

Death as a reunion: One patient made three suicide attempts over a period of some 20 to 25 years. When seen for the first time, following her third suicide attempt, she was 47 years old. Each attempt had been more serious than the one before and she was particularly fortunate to survive the last one, in which she used gas. An unhappy love affair was time-related to all three attempts. After two months of treatment following the third attempt, during which her last love affair continued unsuccessfully, the patient became acutely suicidal and required admission to the hospital. That night she had the following dream. "I was in Baltimore in an apartment where I lived twenty-five years ago. There were a lot of people around who told me to put on a beautiful wedding dress hanging on the wall, but I would not put it on."

Her associations were to the Baltimore apartment where her first romantic liaison had lasted for two years until one night her lover told her he was going to marry another girl. She thereupon made a suicide attempt, and everything in the dream was the same as it had been at the time of her first attempt. In the wedding ceremonies preceding her two unhappy marriages she had failed to wear a wedding dress although she had always wanted to. She felt she had lost the really great love of her life with the end of this first relationship. What impressed her most in the dream was that the wedding dress "looked more like a shroud than like a wedding dress." Apparently union with her first lover was to be achieved only through her death. In fact, the patient recalled that she had had this dream recurrently before each suicide attempt—an interesting detail.

She was, in her dream, refusing to put on the dress while struggling, in reality, against suicide. Death was the unpleasant price she had to pay for the gratification of her desire for love and affection. In other patients with similar but more masochistic psychodynamics, the act of dying itself can be conceived as pleasurably incorporated into the reunion fantasy. Most frequently the emphasis is not placed on the dying but on the gratification to follow, with the mood in such reunion dreams being quite pleasant. In the overwhelming majority the gratification is of an extremely dependent variety, either directly with parental figures or with wives, husbands or siblings substituting as parents.

While such fantasies are usually unconscious and have to be elicited from dreams, they can also be conscious. One patient was seen following a suicide attempt which eventually proved to be fatal. He had been preoccupied for the entire year after his wife's death with fantasies about her and with mental pictures of being reunited with her in death.

Death as rebirth: A young intelligent woman in her twenties, well educated and successful in her work, jumped under a train and lost a leg. Her suicide attempt was precipitated by one of the unhappy and complicated love relationships with which her life had been filled. Several years earlier she had been intensely involved with a married Negro. A few years before that affair she had been in love with a Communist under investigation by the FBI who was at that time trying to use his relationship with her to get into the United States. When she was 13 years old, her father had deserted the family and she had never seen or heard from him again. She had been fascinated by death and dying all through adolescence and always remembered by heart death scenes in novels. Under hypnosis and with the suggestion to have a dream about her suicide attempt, she produced the following. She was in a long, narrow tunnel and could see a light at the end of it. She walked toward the light and there she saw a man and woman standing over a manger. In her associations to the dream the tunnel suggested to her the subway from which she jumped and the way in which the train came out of the tunnel and into the lighted platform area. Moving from the darkness of the tunnel into light brought to her mind the process of birth. The man and woman she saw as her mother and father. The child in the manger was both the Christ child and herself. One can see how much she accomplished in her death fantasy. She is reborn, is a boy, is reunited with her father and finally, she is omnipotent. For a patient with such fantasies the thought of dying has a very strong appeal.

Death as self-punishment: A lawyer in his thirties made a moderately serious suicide attempt which he blamed on his lack of success in a legal career. He could not be hypnotized during his stay in the hospital following his suicide attempt, exemplifying the difficulties encountered if one attempted the routine use of hypnosis for the evaluation of all psychiatric patients. When he returned for a second try, he was relatively easy to hypnotize. He later admitted that he was afraid of hypnosis while both in the hospital and actively preoccupied with suicide. He assumed that if he revealed material related to his wish to die he would not be discharged.

His dreams under hypnosis were of the most elemental kind. In one instance they revealed him running to catch a boat and just missing it. In his associations "missing the boat" symbolized the low opinion which he had of his entire career. His legal ambitions were excessive and he found it impossible to compromise with his grandiose success fantasies. The aggressiveness which stemmed from this grandiosity interfered with his actual performance, a constellation frequently observed in male patients with extremely high and rigid standards for themselves. What is seen as failure causes an enormous degree of self-hatred, and suicide amounts to a self-inflicted punishment for having failed.

Many male patients in this group demonstrated evidence of a paranoid personality structure before they became depressed or suicidal. A typical example was a 55 year old stock broker who was depressed to the extent that he had been unable to work for several years prior to his suicide attempt and my subsequent examination of him. Previously he had a career spanning 30 years, although he had changed positions every two or three years. Every time he claimed to have been the victim of mistreatment, personal favoritism or corruption. Eventually a combination of these factors and his daughter's breakdown proved too much for his paranoid defenses, resulting in the manifestation of his latent depression of long standing. He now began to blame himself and his unworthiness for the failure in his work and bemoaned his misfortune with his daughter. Under psychotherapy he became paranoid toward the writer; significantly, at the same time his depression lifted considerably so that within a few months he could resume his work. With his paranoid defenses re-activated, his depressive symptomatology lessened and he became able to function.

This type of suicidal self-punishment reaction over failure at work has not been observed in women. A suicidal self-punishment reaction that can be seen in women was illustrated by the previously mentioned patient who was unable to love her child. When a woman's inability to love her child is accompanied by the expectation that she should feel what she is not feeling, strong self-hatred with the need for self-punishment can be the result.

A variation of the view of suicide as self-punishment which occurs in patients of either sex may be illustrated in the following case. A 30 year old man from a relatively stable rural family as the sixth of eight children felt "superfluous" from early childhood. While all the other siblings were married and apparently leading responsible lives, he considered himself the black sheep of the family. From the age of 18 he was a moderately severe alcoholic. His "impossible" marriage resulted likewise in feelings of being "superfluous" and quickly ended in divorce. His main occupation had been that of a seaman, but his explosive temper and frequent fights aboard ship led to unemployment and depressed feelings. He reported the following dream which he had immediately prior to an impulsive suicide attempt (jumping in front of a moving car). "An atom bomb was falling . . . I was in hell and about to be burned. My brother was above, saying that I should be burned." The patient believed that he would end up in hell if he did not lead "a more Christian life." Eight months earlier he had begun to attend church in order to force himself to live differently, but without success. His extremely religious mother was opposed to drinking, smoking or any amusement for its own sake. Although he had never been close to her, he had taken over her religious beliefs despite his inability to live up to them. The brother in the dream was the family member closest to the patient; nevertheless, their relation had been characterized by fights and reconciliations until the time of his brother's death three years earlier.

During the previous eight years the patient had made several impulsive suicide attempts, including one where he jumped in front of a moving jeep and was severely injured. Suicide was for him an act of atonement, and death a fair punishment for his explosiveness, his anger toward his siblings and the world, and for his asocial life.

Among the most disturbed suicidal patients of both sexes seen in mental hospitals, feelings of being worthless predominate, and self-punishment is a prominent feature. The original motivation may be centered around failure, guilt over aggression or attempted expiation; however, the self-punishment may be dissociated from these goals and thus become almost an end in itself. Such patients tend to be preoccupied with delusional feelings of guilt, sin and unworthiness.

The patient who sees himself as already dead: One man jumped in front of a train and lost one leg almost to the hip as well as an arm. Some months later he related a dream in which he was shopping for a coffin. The coffin maker told him that his coffin was only half-finished. In view of the fact that he had lost two limbs in his suicide attempt, the dream seemed to project a current picture of himself. His associations to the dream indicated that in his opinion only his physical death was half completed. Emotionally, however, he felt that he had died years before making any suicide attempt.

One very withdrawn suicidal girl of 18 had a recurrent nightmare in which she saw dry ice coming closer and closer to her. It threatened to envelop her until she woke up in panic. She was tormented by her inability "to feel anything for anyone." Not only did she feel dead, but her physical appearance and motility suggested a kind of walking death. The dry ice image was a self-image—a self that was seen as permanently frozen, dangerous to others, and self-destructive.

Patients of this kind are representative of an entire group preoccupied with the feeling of being already dead, generally not in a delusional sense but in the sense of being emotionally dead. Strong feelings of detachment, repressed aggression and dampened affectivity are perceived by many patients as the equivalent of emotional dying or death. Clinically, these patients may appear apathetic rather than depressed, and their suicide attempts rarely change this mood. Despite overt apathy, such deadness is experienced by suicidal patients as extremely torturous, so that they see suicide either as a release from suffering or as merely carrying out an event which has already happened.

✻   ✻   ✻

In summary, an attempt has been made in this chapter to demonstrate some of the psychodynamic patterns seen in suicidal patients in connection with different fantasies and attitudes toward death. Seven such patterns have been outlined and illustrated: death as abandonment, death as omnipotent mastery, death as retroflexed murder, death as a reunion, death as rebirth, death as self-punishment or atonement, and death as a phenomenon that in an emotional sense has already taken place.

The death fantasy of the suicidal individual is not simply helpful in revealing his motivation for suicide, but is also integrally a part of his entire attitude toward life as well as death. The individual who expects his suicide and death to continue a punishment which he deserves is quite different from the individual who hopes for the gratification of dependent desires in a protected reunion with a maternal figure. They reveal quite different character structures and not merely different suicidal psychodynamics. Death fantasies thus come to serve as a natural aid in distinguishing the various motivational psychodynamics seen in suicide.

Differences in the fantasies about suicide, death and afterlife will be seen to have their importance in the three Scandinavian countries and to reflect differences in the psychosocial character of the respective countries. With the psychodynamics of suicide as a background we can now turn to suicide in Scandinavia.

CHAPTER IV

Suicide in Denmark

DENMARK lends itself well to a study of psychosocial character. Although the rural areas of Jutland and Zealand are as different from Copenhagen as rural Iowa is from New York City, Denmark is more homogeneous in her traditions, institutions and attitudes than the hybrid and diversified population of the United States.*

Fortunately, from the standpoint of this study, a high percentage of the Danish people, including those of limited general education, speak English well, English having been a compulsory language there from early school years for about 25 years.† Consequently I was able to study 25 suicidal patients as well as five non-suicidal inpatients and five non-suicidal outpatients. The language situation was also advantageous for the psychoanalytic form of the interviewing technique and its reliance as much on what the patient unwittingly revealed as on what he actually said. Interviews with five other patients who were seen with a psychiatric colleague serving as interpreter were much less fruitful. The spontaneous sequence and flow of the patients' associations were lost—the essence of the advantage inherent in interviews of a psychoanalytic nature. And perhaps my own relative unfamiliarity with the institutions and attitudes of the country turned out to be more of an advantage than a disad-

---

* This relative homogeneity in comparison to the United States is true of Norway and Sweden as well. This fact, together with the small population in each country (4.7 million in Denmark, 7.5 million in Sweden and 3.6 million in Norway), makes them excellent sources for the study of the effect of different institutions and attitudes on psychosocial character.

† Widespread use of English as the first foreign language is more recent in Sweden and Norway. In preliminary visits to these two countries I realized that, except among the educated, there was not the knowledge of English that I had found in Denmark and that fluency in Norwegian and Swedish would be necessary in order to continue my work.

vantage. Every day I was struck by attitudes in patients which were remarkably different from those in the United States, but which might have been taken for granted or overlooked had I spent my life in Denmark.

For example, one afternoon at the Copenhagen Military Hospital I heard a young Danish soldier, who had made a suicide attempt, threatening his Danish psychiatrist that he would commit suicide if he were returned to camp. When the doctor doubted that the boy would actually kill himself, the latter replied that the doctor could not, in fact, be certain and that if he did kill himself, his death would be on the doctor's conscience.

Such incidents are common in Denmark, since suicidal threats are often used by Danish boys who want to get out of the army. Not that American boys want to get out of service any the less, but how different is the means they are likely to employ. Vague psychosomatic complaints or difficult-to-diagnose syndromes (including, for instance, the famous low back pain) are probably the most common, while suicide threats are relatively infrequent. The American boy assumes that the threat of suicide will be futile, for he does not expect to be taken seriously. As a rule, he is right in this assumption. The Danish soldier, on the other hand, can be quite certain that threats of this kind will arouse immediate concern and anxiety among his comrades and superiors. In the United States suicide threats occur less frequently among soldiers than among civilians. To be effective, a threat must have a receiver, and among Americans such threats are usually directed at mothers, fathers, wives and husbands. The American sergeant is none of these.

On another afternoon a rather sick Danish girl talked to me about her childhood and later life. Suddenly she stopped and said that she could go no further because to do so would only make me feel guilty. Why should it make me feel guilty? Well, she said, because I probably had a happier childhood and I would feel guilty on that account. I assured her that since I did not feel responsible for her unhappy childhood, I would not feel guilty—that, at most, I might only feel fortunate to have escaped whatever she had gone through. She was then able to continue. But what was this girl doing? She obviously wanted me to feel guilty, and then felt guilty herself for this wish. What a refined and sophisticated psychology of guilt! This girl's behavior and that of the Danish soldier could be reiterated in a number of similar illustrations and were indicative of an extraordinary ability to arouse guilt in others through one's own suffering or misfortune; the expectation of being able to do so has important bearing on the whole question of suicide.

It also raises the question as to how this behavior is learned. Does the Danish mother use the arousal of guilt as a disciplinary technique and, if so, how often? It is one of many kinds of discipline that can be used with children. It is in fact used by many subcultures within the United States, and no one can be certain of its effectiveness in comparison with other forms of discipline.

From interviews with Danish patients and many talks with Danish mothers and Danish psychiatrists, it may be concluded that this is the principal form of discipline used in Denmark. The mother simply lets the child know how hurt she is and how badly she feels at his (or her) behavior. The child is thereby disciplined—and at the same time receives a lesson in the technique of arousing guilt which he can later put to his own uses.

Discussion of the problem of guilt opens the whole question of aggression and how it is handled, expressed or controlled. In general, far less overt destructiveness or violence is observed among Danish patients than will be seen among American patients. A disturbed ward in a Danish hospital is altogether a far quieter place than a similar ward in one of our hospitals, and patients on such a Danish ward are more apt to be quiet than actively enraged and throwing things. The strikingly low Danish homicide rate, in comparison with the American, is also relevant here. In a recent year there were only 28 homicides in the entire country, 13 of whom were children killed by their parents in connection with their own suicide.

This control of aggression begins, of course, in childhood. The Danish child, while indulged in many ways, is not permitted to show the aggression toward his parents and siblings that is tolerated in an American child. Consequently Danish children impress Americans as exceedingly well-disciplined and well-behaved, while some American children may seem like monsters to the Danes.

If there is, by the way, a socially acceptable outlet for aggression among the Danes, it is their sense of humor. They are very fond of teasing and are proud of their wit. Their humor will often cloak aggressive barbs in such a manner as to get the point across without actually provoking open friction.

A great deal has been written with regard to suicide about the importance of aggression turned inward. Yet, as indicated in earlier chapters, it is far from being the whole story about suicide in general and equally far from being the whole story about suicide in Denmark. The English, for example, who also curb aggression in their children, have a low homicide rate without the high Danish suicide rate.

What is apparently basic to the Danish vulnerability to depression and suicide is the unique forms of dependence seen in Denmark. As one Danish psychiatrist stated, you can, in a way, divide the Danes into two groups: those who are looking for someone to take care of them and those who are looking for someone to take care of. There is a good deal of truth in this epigram.

Here, too, it is best to begin with the child. The Danish child's dependence on his mother is encouraged far more than that of the American child. Danish mothers are apt to boast of how well their children look, how well they eat, and how much they weigh. They are far less likely to boast of those activities or qualities of the child that in any way tend to separate him from the mother; how fast the child can walk or talk or do things by himself. The child is fondled and coddled more often and babied until a later age than is generally true in the United States. The American mother may not curb her child's aggressiveness because she may fear damaging his initiative. Since the Danish mother is less ruled by this concern, the child's aggressiveness is strictly checked —is, in a sense, part of the price he pays for his dependence. Of course, the very checking of the child's aggressiveness serves, in turn, to increase and foster this dependence. Such a behavior pattern will make the separation from the mother, when it does come, all the harder to bear. Many Danes seek a return to the maternal relationship either directly or through a mother-substitute, while others achieve this kind of gratification vicariously— through attending to the dependent needs of others.

Of course, combinations and variations are common. Characteristic was the attitude of a 22 year old Danish girl who was unable to manage her life in Copenhagen. She yearned to return to her parents' farm in northern Zealand and wanted to be taken care of by her mother. In the next breath she expressed the idea that perhaps the solution to her problem was to go to England and live with a young artist, since she had found on a recent visit that he was totally helpless and needed her.

The checking of aggression and the encouragement of dependency also lead to the frequently observed character attitude of passivity. In comparing depressed, suicidal or non-suicidal male patients in Denmark with corresponding groups in the United States, one is impressed with the number of Danish patients who exhibit extreme degrees of passivity. The Danes also accept their passivity, often good-naturedly and certainly without the anxiety and conflict one sees in passive American patients. Typical was the remark of a young man of 28 who was dissatisfied with his work as a ship's cook and said: "Everyone tells me I should change my job, but no one tells me how to do it."

This passivity is reflected in the work of the distinguished contemporary Danish cartoonist, Robert Storm Petersen. He satirizes the machine age through fantastically complicated inventions for flicking the ashes from a cigar or for opening a soda bottle. His American counterpart with equally fantastic inventions is Rube Goldberg whose recent cartoon book was entitled *How to Get the Cotton out of a Bottle of Aspirin.* But how different is their treatment of the same idea! The Petersen cartoons invariably show the central male figure being served by machines while the male sits or lies in positions which satirize the extremes of man's passivity. In the Goldberg cartoons the central male is usually a frantic part of the complex invention which causes him a thousand times more work than it saves him.

The search for dependence results in greater need of the sexes for each other, and in a more pronounced willingness of the sexes to move toward each other with less fear and more ease than is usual in the United States. Marriage involves many economic sacrifices and often takes place when a child is expected. There is less pressure on the unmarried to get married, and, as a consequence, less panic in girls of 23 to 28 who are unmarried than one sees in the United States. Mutual attraction is not impeded by the intense competition between the sexes that is so common in the United States. Of course, since such expectations of dependent gratification from the opposite sex are often disappointed, they are a major cause for separations and divorces.* As one divorced woman said of her husband and some other men whom she subsequently met: "Men are looking for sex and I am looking for a man to take care of me and give me a pat on the back."

Within the family, the pattern of the passive father and forceful mother is seen more and more distinctly. Danish preoccupation with evidence for this pattern in the United States is partly a reflection of their own anxieties about it. One patient who spoke of the submissiveness of men to women in the United States had all his life been ruled by his wife.

The position of the Danish husband often resembles that of a privileged oldest child. He is rarely concerned with the discipline

---

* Rudfeld[1] and Pærregaard[2] in Denmark have independently stressed the dramatically high frequency of suicide among the separated and divorced, and there is justification for doing so.

Care, however, must be taken to avoid the pitfall of assuming that frequent separation and divorce provide any kind of explanation for the high Danish suicide rate. If one takes the year 1956 that Rudfeld worked with as an example and subtracts all the suicides committed by separated and divorced people from the total suicide figure, the Danish rate drops only from 22.4 to 19.4. Or if one takes the female suicide rate alone, it drops only from 15.4 to 13.4 when separated and divorced female suicides are subtracted from the total. This subtraction has so little relative effect because by far the greatest number of suicides, male and female, fall into the married class even though the probability is greater for a given individual who is separated or divorced. Thus, when all is said and done, the Danish suicide rate is high because the suicide rate of the married population is high, and this population most determines the rate. A careful reading of Durkheim shows he was aware of the deceptive nature of the figures for suicide among the divorced. He cautioned against the danger of being led away from the less striking but more significant figures for the married into thinking that increased divorce was essentially responsible for a rise in suicide or that its prevention would be curative.

The high Danish divorce rate (considerably higher than that of Norway) is important in itself as an indicator of difficulties in the relationship between the sexes. The particular psychodynamic patterns seen in Danish suicide point to the same conclusion, but the psychodynamic study of the patients has the advantage of making possible some definition of the sources of the difficulty.

of the children. Resentment on the part of fathers at the birth of children is quite common, being most strikingly evidenced in the common observation of Danish psychotherapists of loss of potency or loss of sexual interest on the husband's part after the birth of the first child.

Many of the suicidal women complained that their own dependent longings had interfered with their functioning as mothers and wives. Their inability to care more adequately for their children played an important role in their attempted suicide. With an openness that was both appealing and yet almost childlike in manner, male and female patients spoke of having been too egocentric to care deeply for anyone. Complaints of emotional emptiness were frequent. Several patients said that they only took something from people without giving anything back. Interestingly, these patients remembered with much guilt that they had actually stolen from their mothers when they were children. This observation seemed to prove, if such proof were needed, that the overprotected child was far from being a satisfied one.

One woman who had often thought of leaving her husband did not do so because of her youngest child. The night before her suicide attempt she dreamt that she was unable to take a picture of her family because the youngest child repeatedly ran out of the visual field. She kept on chasing after him and became tired. She was clearly struggling against her wish to have the child out of the picture in order to be able to do what she planned. She had not wanted to have this last child and had overreacted to his birth by being more concerned and protective toward him than she had been toward her first two children.

This conflict over caring for children was expressed in other ways by non-suicidal patients. One woman was obsessed with the thought that she might kill her children. She was going again and again through rituals to prevent such a calamity. During one of our last interviews she reported the following dream: she had given birth to a baby. Then she was making out forms for merchandise to obtain a ten per cent discount on them. By this time she was able to see for herself what she wished to express in the dream: her desire to get rid of her baby and at a profit.

Frigidity among Danish women appears to be as widespread as it is in the United States. This is the case despite their very feminine manner, their relative non-competitiveness with men, and the fact that they have somewhat more sexual freedom during adolescence than Americans, though no more during childhood. (The attitude of Danish mothers toward sexual activity in their children is generally to prohibit it and at the same time to deny its existence—very much as American mothers do.) Yet female frigidity does not appear to be of the guilt-ridden type common in the United States 30 years ago, or of the competitive type common today. It seems to be caused by the woman's dependent longings and by her image of herself as a little girl rather than as a grown woman.

This marked dependency concern alone can explain the Danes' extreme vulnerability to depression and suicide following the ending of relationships. Both the protector and the protected will be vulnerable in such a situation. Typical was the attitude of one man who made a serious suicide attempt when his wife left him after 20 years of marriage. He complained that his wife was very cold sexually, very possessive, and always nagging and scolding. He drank heavily over the past ten years and thereby precipitated his wife's leaving. He felt lost without her. Although she came in to clean for him once a week, he had no desire to live because there was no one to prepare his meals and attend to his needs. He had a tobacco shop that he ran together with his wife and now was unable to handle alone. It had been 18 years earlier that the patient's mother died of cancer, but he became tearful during the interview when he talked about her death. Twice during the course of our sessions he slipped, referring to his wife as his mother.

In a suicide note to his wife he said only that he was sorry for making her unhappy and bade goodbye to his daughter. He did not deny that he was angry with his wife inasmuch as she had no right to leave him. He doubted, however, that his suicide attempt was in any way an expression of this anger, since his wife would be better off with his pension. When challenged about the contradiction between his anger and his wish for her to be better off, he became quite irritated. He justified his resigned attitude toward life in general by saying that at the age of 52 it was too late for him to find anyone else or do anything different with his life. He had lived in the United States and Canada for a year prior to his marriage and expressed the belief that possibly because of better food the people there were stronger and more vigorous until a later period in life.

Consistent with this dependency pattern is a far greater prevalence of depression as the presenting symptom in psychiatric patients than is seen in the United States. Of course, many of the Danish patients with presumably endogenous or psychogenic depressions would have been classified as schizophrenic in this country. Nevertheless, an American psychiatrist cannot fail to be impressed by the predominance of depressive symptoms even in patients categorized here as schizophrenic.

For example, one very depressed 33 year old woman blamed a suicide attempt on her inability to love either her husband or her two young children. In her own opinion, she had never felt anything for anyone and had always lived "with her brain." In particular, it was on intellectual grounds that she had decided to marry and have children because "it was the thing to do." Various aspects of her history (the likelihood of recovery from her current depression, and the fact that she had only recently spoken to her husband or anyone else about her incapacity for love) were interpreted by the Danish psychiatrists as evidence of a depression, although some of her main symptoms (inability to feel anything for anyone and the tendency to copy personal relationships intellectually) could be traced to her adolescence and would have been regarded here as typical features of schizophrenia. However, what is really more important is the fact that even in patients who would be diagnosed as schizophrenic in the United States it is frequently the depressive symptomatology that brings them to psychiatric attention in Denmark.

*   *   *

Mention has been made of the manipulation of guilt, the control of aggression, and the various forms of dependency. Of particular interest in relation to the subject of dependency are the Danish attitudes toward death and afterlife as well as toward suicide itself.

In working with suicidal patients in the United States, one encounters fantasies of reunion after death with a lost loved one. In Denmark, however, such fantasies are so much more common as to be almost the rule. This observation was striking in view of the fact that most of the Danes in this study tended to stress their "not being religious" with an overtone of pride. Yet, the Lutheran concept of an afterlife is universally taught in the schools, and many children are introduced to the idea of reunion after death by their parents before they go to school. Even when interest in formal religion diminishes in later life, fantasies of an afterlife and of reunion with loved ones after death are usually maintained. These ideas are not only more prevalent in Danish than in American patients, but they are more openly expressed; with most American patients they have to be ascertained from dreams. The predominance of these ideas is also consistent with the Danish dependency constellation.

One Danish patient with such a fantasy was interviewed following a serious suicide attempt with gas. He was a 56 year old man who had been separated from his wife for several months. During the interview he expressed the idea that after his death he expected to be reunited with his mother who had died eight years earlier—and eventually, upon his wife's death, with his wife. He doubted that he and his wife would have marital difficulties in their afterlives similar to those they had had on earth. He claimed to have believed in the concept of an afterlife since his first school years or before. When asked if he had not been taught that suicide would preclude his going to heaven, he acknowledged having been taught this doctrine, but expressed doubts as to its validity. In his opinion, everything would be forgiven if one repented. His last act before turning on the gas had been to say a prayer in which he asked forgiveness for what he was about to do; with that, he felt confident that his admission to an afterlife was assured. His attitudes in these matters turned out to be quite typical of Danish patients.

In general, ideas of this kind could be consciously elicited from patients during the interviews. However, one or two instances in which the patient's dreams affirmed his conscious attitude may serve to clarify the point.

A 56 year old woman had taken 30 barbiturate tablets shortly before Christmas, approximately eight months after the deaths of both her father and the man she had lived with for ten years. She believed in a life after death and expected to find both men there. Following her suicide attempt and admission to the hospital, she dreamed that she was at a Christmas party, with all the people present being strangers.

In her associations to the dream she explained that Christmas used to be the time when she went home to visit her family. This year she had to go home at Christmas time for her father's burial. Although there were only strangers at the Christmas party, she had not been unhappy in her dream. From the time of her hospital admission she had been telling herself that she would have to live out her life. The dream was interpreted by her in terms of her desire to be united with her family because of her loneliness as well as an attempt to deny these feelings and to accept the fact that she might even be able to be happy with strangers.

A 20 year old Danish girl was admitted to the hospital because of a suicide attempt in which she impulsively jumped in front of a car which barely managed to stop before hitting her. Shortly after her admission she had a dream in which she threw herself under the train at Valby. In some unexplained manner she was hooked by the train and taken to Copenhagen. While everybody left the train on one side, she got off on the other and found herself near a place where bicycles were shipped to the city.

Her associations were as follows: Valby was located between Copenhagen and the town where her parents lived. It was linked in her mind with her visits home, because she had often stopped there on the way. Throwing herself in front of the train recalled an English story about a woman who had thrown herself in front of a car in Piccadilly Circus. She had never been in the bicycle store because she had not taken her bicycle to Copenhagen, having been afraid of the traffic in the city. This portion of the dream, as well as the part in which she left the train on the wrong side, was related to her inability to cope with city life and to her feeling of isolation from the rest of the people there. Her suicidal act was seen plainly as an unsuccessful attempt to be reunited with her parents. Her failure meant that she had to remain in the city or be dragged into the city against her will. Although she believed in an afterlife, she consciously wanted to return to the protective care of her parents without the necessity of dying. However, she did not think that her parents would permit her to return home; hence reunion with them would be possible only after death.

Apart from individual dreams, the most perceptive prototypes of such reunion-in-death fantasies can be found in that singular Danish literature, the fairy tales of Hans Christian Andersen.[3] There is The Little Match Girl who, while freezing to death in the cold, lights her matches and sees the image of her grandmother, the only person who ever loved her and with whom she is reunited after her death. There is The Steadfast Tin Soldier who can be united with the ballerina doll only through the fire that destroys them. The Andersen stories are full of these fantasies of death, dying and afterlife. Suicide itself is treated almost openly in The Old Street Lamp. Fearful of decomposition, the lamp is relieved of this fear when it obtains the power of self-destruction, so to speak, by turning to rust in one day. (Many suicidal patients, as was noted in the chapter dealing with the psychodynamics of suicide, have a feeling of mastery over all kinds of anxieties including a fear of death, because they can end their lives at will.) The lamp finally decides against using this power. Despite a preference for a new existence, the lamp decides not to seek it, since there are others (the watchman and his wife) who need it and are to be considered.

Fantasies of rebirth are often associated with reunion after death. The Ugly Duckling represents the idea that while one may be unloved and unwanted in this life, one's future existence may be quite different; thus the duckling is "reborn" as a swan. There is no reference to dying in the story, but the psychological meaning of being reborn is evident.

On the whole, the love-death theme—the idea that without love there will be death, although the desire for love may be gratified in death—runs through the Andersen stories. The boy who is in bondage to The Snow Queen is emotionally frozen. He has a "heart like ice" and can obtain pleasure only in reason. Only through the strength of little Gerda's love and faith can he be returned to normal.

It should be pointed out here that these are by no means the universal themes of all fairy tales. Only consider that in the Andersen tales competition and superhuman performance are not depicted as important. Neither giants nor dragons have to be killed in order for the hero to succeed in whatever he is up to.

To be sure, the subject of death is as taboo in Denmark as it is in the United States, if not more so. Parents are uncomfortable when their children mention it. The Danes do not use funerals as an occasion for grief or mourning; they find them painful and want them to be over as soon as possible. Being uncomfortable around a bereaved person, they aim at shortening the period of grieving and then wish the subject to be dropped. And such discomfort is in keeping with their anxiety about separation, loss or abandonment by a source of dependency gratification. Several Danish psychiatrists, psychologists and sociologists expressed the idea that a longer period of grieving would probably be salutary, acting as a kind of safety valve.

Suicide itself is less taboo in Denmark than it is in the United States, and much less than in Catholic countries. Patients who have made a suicide attempt seem to be less ashamed than are such patients in the United States. The Danish patient may express shame at not having actually completed the act rather than at having made the attempt. His spouse may present some evidence of shame, but the general attitude of those around the patient is more likely to be one of sympathy or pity. Early religious references to suicide as an immoral act do not appear to have a strong hold on people—a fact stressed by an experienced Danish clergyman in a personal communication. Moreover, with so many Danes having relatives or friends who have killed themselves or made suicide attempts, any taboo related to self-destruction is bound to be weakened. Suicide need not be institutionalized, as it is in Japan, in order to become a virtually acceptable expression of unhappiness.

Emphasis has been put on distinctive features in Danish psychosocial character. But it is certainly true that any one of the Danish patterns may also be found in the United States. American patients of English extraction or Puritan heritage tend to exercise rigid control over the expression of aggression. At the same time, however, they discourage feelings of excessive dependency.

Many patients with a southern or eastern European background use the arousal of guilt to express hostility or to enforce compliance with their wishes; but, just as characteristically, they do not suppress aggression as do the Danes. It is apparently a combination of the various traits mentioned that makes the Danes liable to attempt suicide rather than to discharge aggression and frustration in some other way.

In summary, the particular Danish vulnerability to the loss of dependency should again be stressed. The most common situation which may precipitate a suicidal act is such a dependency loss through death, separation or divorce, or most often through the deterioration of a personal relationship. Combined with this dependency, and reinforcing it, is the Danish tendency to control and suppress aggression. Moreover, there is the learned familiarity with the use of personal suffering as a technique for arousing guilt in others and insuring desired gratification. The patterned control of aggression and the use of guilt-arousing techniques expedite the use of suicide as a method of dealing with the frustration and anger generated by dependency loss. Mention should also be made of the frequency of fantasies concerning gratification after death—a frequency that is consistent with the dependency desires—and of the lesser degree of shame attached to the suicidal act in the Danish culture.

This appraisal does not mean that every social or characterological pattern playing a role in the psychodynamics of suicide in general plays a significant role in Danish suicide. The study of suicidal attempts throws light on particular anxieties and preoccupations of the people in a given country, and it is to be expected that there will be many variations from country to country. It would seem to be significant, for instance, that one particular background factor common elsewhere is rarely observed among the Danes.

The pattern referred to as having little bearing on the Danish suicide rate is organized around performance and competitiveness. If only because of Denmark's proximity to, and previous political control of some districts by, Germany, special attention was paid to the frequently described Germanic overconscientiousness about performance. In line with this pattern, the individual has rather ambitious and rigid expectations of himself, and a great deal of aggression is tied up with the achievement of these expectations. Failure of achievement in this kind of culture can be a direct cause of suicidal acts. Likewise, the failure to achieve love will not be interpreted, as in the Danish culture, as an emotional deprivation, but primarily as a poor performance in which the individual gives himself, so to speak, a low mark in love.

It has already been noted that competitiveness and performance do not figure significantly in the fairy tales of Hans Christian Andersen, while in the German folklore the conquest of giants and dragons is crucial, and the winning of the heroine may be more or less incidental. In the light of what has been said about Danish family life, upbringing and general attitudes, it would not seem surprising that such a performance pattern does not have the same life-and-death meaning in Denmark that it appears to have in Germany and Switzerland and probably in Japan as well.

Although the Danish child experiences a fair share of competition in school, he is not particularly encouraged by his family to be competitive. It is generally understood by both children and adults that no one should stand out too much in any direction. This attitude is by no means unknown among Americans, but it is more intense among the Danes. Anyone violating this rule against conspicuously high performance, whether it be the child in school or the adult at work, is subject to a good deal of envy and dislike.

What is the importance then of the Danish social welfare system[4] in fostering the national attitudes toward competition and dependency? Apparently most of these characteristics antedated the social and economic changes which occurred during the last few decades. What can be said is that the welfare system may reinforce, and provide an outlet for, these qualities and attitudes in the national character, which in turn may be expected to shape the particular form that social change has taken. Governmental concern for the individual gives some permission for the overt expression of the desire to be taken care of. Even the tone of many letters to Danish newspapers indicates a feeling of passively endured injustice, particularly under conditions of economic difficulty, thus reflecting a lesser feeling of responsibility for one's personal destiny than is customary here.

Numerous social welfare agencies provide an opportunity for those who wish to care for the dependent needs of others. On the whole, there is a greater concern in Denmark than in the United States on the part of those administering the help—whether it be medical care or financial aid—with the welfare of everyone. Also, there is an almost universal tendency to feel personally responsible for the suffering of others. In discussing this tendency at a seminar in Copenhagen, one doctor stated by way of illustration (and others agreed) that virtually everyone might feel guilt or responsibility in reading a newspaper account of a deceased man whose body went undiscovered in his room for several days. The general assumption would be that he was lonely, uncared for, and probably without friends. But this is all a far cry from equating the welfare state with suicide. As noted in the first chapter, the Danish suicide rate has been high for a period long antedating the social welfare measures, while despite highly developed social welfare measures[5] the suicide rate in Norway is particularly low.

With its lack of natural resources, it is difficult to visualize Denmark as wealthy under any economic system. Even were Denmark to lean toward more capitalistic practices, there would not be much wealth for her to capitalize. Nor could Denmark be expected to survive in the competitive international economy without a greater degree of internal economic cooperation and planning than is considered necessary here. Both the limited wealth within the country and the high taxes required for social welfare activities restrict the accumulation of wealth by individual Danish families. These limitations have shifted the emphasis toward status and position as sources of prestige. In medicine, for instance, hospital position and rank are considerably more important than they are here. Hence they present an entirely different value for the career and aspirations of the Danish physician, especially since in a country that has not expanded economically and in population as rapidly as ours, the number of top positions is obviously limited.

A consequence of these limitations may have been a lessening of competition. In an effort to improve one's economic situation, individual initiative would have accomplished less here than it might have, for example, in the United States or in Denmark's wealthier neighbor, Sweden.

Thus, although economic life seems more difficult, Denmark has managed to escape some of the pressure of the continuous chase for wealth and material goods that prevails in the rest of the Western world. One can observe within a short time that the pace of life in Copenhagen is slower than that in cities like New York or Stockholm.

CHAPTER V

Suicide in Sweden

Since "reserved" is the adjective used so often by natives as well as by foreigners to describe the Swedes, more difficulty was anticipated in establishing initial contacts with the patients than was experienced in Denmark. And in fact, the patients did show greater reserve in dealing with their emotional problems. It would often take several hours to obtain the type of cooperation that the Danish patient gave from the beginning.

In the Swedish women a common reaction to being interviewed a second or third time was to express embarrassment at having revealed so much about themselves. This attitude contrasted with that of the Danish women, who usually stated in their second interview that they had thought of many other things which they were now eager to report. The Swedish women blush frequently—and by blush is meant a full facial reddening from the top of the forehead right down to the neck. The blush was precipitated by any expression of inner feelings during the interview and usually was a reaction to this exposure rather than to any specific subject matter. Actually the blushing seemed indicative of the desire to reveal feelings as well as of the embarrassment caused by this desire.

On the whole, the men were somewhat harder to reach emotionally than were the women. They seldom were spontaneously talkative, and in facial expression and body movement they tended to be constrained.* When questioned about their feelings, they were often defensive or cooperated with an attitude of intellectual curiosity rather than with emotional involvement. Being

---

* A popular reflection of the male tendency toward silence and stiffness is found in the work of one of Sweden's leading contemporary cartoonists, Salon Gahlin. His male figures are consistently drawn with rigid bodies, and their mouths are usually miniscule, hidden by a mustache or omitted entirely.

clearly status-conscious, they were inclined to be deferential toward doctors to a somewhat exaggerated degree and in a way that interfered with easy emotional expression. However, when these initial barriers were overcome, the men proved to be in much poorer contact with their own feelings than were the women. They showed evidence of emotional reactions to wives, parents, employers or friends, but seemed unaware of these reactions. Particularly difficult for them was the open expression of anger or a frank criticism of anyone in their immediate surroundings.

Fortunately it was possible to see the patients as many times as was deemed necessary for an adequate psychodynamic appraisal, usually requiring 5 to 25 sessions. Seeing the patients was facilitated by the fact that I was able to observe 25 suicidal patients at one hospital—Södersjukhuset in Stockholm. Most of the patients were seen during their stay in the hospital following a suicide attempt and then subsequently as outpatients. Working primarily in one hospital made it possible for one psychologist to do almost all of the psychological testing. The Rorschach and TAT were administered to 20 of the 25 suicidal patients, so that the clinical findings could be compared with those of the psychologist.

Fifteen other non-suicidal patients were interviewed either at Långbro Hospital or Södersjukhuset and six non-patient nurses were interviewed at Långbro. Ten other suicidal patients were interviewed less intensively at both hospitals. Half of the patients were interviewed in Swedish, and half in English, with virtually the same results for the two groups. All of the nurses were interviewed in Swedish.

※   ※   ※

Early in this study I was impressed by the Swedish male patients' preoccupation with performance and success and by the relationship between these concerns and their suicide attempts. The Swede's ambitiousness and his intensive pursuit of money and material goods seemed as strong as anything seen in the United States, making an American psychiatrist feel at home very soon. At any rate, the intimate relationship between anxiety generated by ambition and attempted suicide was in sharp contrast to what had been seen in Denmark. The Danish men, both old and young, although occasionally referring to work as a problem, were much more concerned about the loss of some love object than they were about work or vocational performance. Some of the Swedish young men (below 35 years), just as young men in Denmark or the United States, were reacting to the loss of a woman; but it is the older men who are the core of the suicide problem in any country. In Sweden men over 35 years of age seldom commit suicide simply over the loss of dependency; it is rather their failure to reach ambitious goals or rigidly defined standards that motivates their suicide.

The observed attitudes would quickly dispel the idea that the social welfare state had destroyed individual initiative and ambition. From a psychological as well as economic standpoint, it should be stressed that added work or added ambition and determination can "pay off" in Sweden. Despite high taxes interfering with the accumulation of great new wealth, additional work by the man or his wife can substantially increase the income of most lower and middle class people, and there are plenty of things for the money to buy—houses, cars, clothes and TV sets. Compared with Denmark, the country is wealthy and abounds in natural resources (water power, timber and iron). Hence there is no lack of incentive for the Swede's ambition, and this fact is bound to play a role in determining his competitive and acquisitive attitudes.

A few illustrations may serve to define the Swedish attitudes toward work and performance and their relation to suicide.

For more than ten years a 55 year old patient, who had never received a desired academic appointment and had to settle for a governmental office job instead, had a recurrent dream. In the dream he was anxiously trying to catch a bus on the corner and missed it. He had this dream twice in connection with suicide attempts and several times when he was particularly upset. Since he attached no significance to the "just-missing-it" quality of the dreams, he wondered why recurring anxiety dreams should be concerned with something so trivial.

The man had worked for five years on a history of the United States. He expected that the volume would do well in Sweden, although its quality had been affected by his excessive drinking habits. Apparently his expectation that the book would finally establish and repair his damaged self-esteem was somewhat on the grandiose side. During our sessions he had the following dream: he was in an elevator with the Crown Prince of Sweden and was taking him to the King. However, the elevator stalled.

His associations dealt with some compliments received on his return to work after the absence necessitated by his suicide attempt. He had also been stimulated by a biography of J. P. Morgan, with whom he liked to identify himself in fantasy. The stalled elevator was related to the way in which his plans for success in life had been stalled. He considered it likely that he was the Crown Prince's teacher in the dream. Although he did not consciously connect the royal family with his own, he kept on talking about his family and expressed the belief that his achievements never measured up to what had been expected of him.

In this patient, as in most of the other suicidal men in Sweden, out-and-out anxiety was a more striking symptom than depression. Such patients would have been diagnosed in this country as having an anxiety depression. As a rule, depressive patients are less active in both psychomotor activity and speech. While Swedish men were not generally talkative, many suicidal patients with severe anxiety or an anxiety depression appeared stimulated by this anxiety into talking more than the usual patient. Absent, too, was the classical psychodynamic pattern of depression characterized by wishes and fantasies of dependent gratification with anger that becomes self-directed—a reaction to the frustration of these wishes. The anxious Swedish male patient did not expect more help from someone else, but tended to redouble his impossible demands on himself. Hence he clearly differed from the Danish patient, in whom clinical depression was the presenting symptom associated with the typical psychodynamic picture of depression. Apart from this difference Danish patients showed far more passivity than their Swedish counterparts, even the ones described as passive in Sweden.

The severe anxiety displayed by the last patient and the majority of the other male suicidal patients in Sweden centered around getting ahead in life or, more commonly, around feelings of frustration over lack of success. Performance and success-failure preoccupations are common in suicidal patients in the United States; so is concern over abandonment and loss. In

Danish men the latter features predominate; in Swedish men, the former. Even in patients with less exalted ambitions than those of our first case anxiety was closely related to work and performance.

A 76 year old man had lost his wife two months before a suicide attempt, seemingly in response to this loss. It was easy to establish, however, that he had made an earlier suicidal attempt a few years before his wife's death. When asked about his life history, he could give a detailed account of his working record from the age of 14 until his recent retirement after the death of his wife. Although he was chiefly a railroad worker, he had also had a shoemaker's shop for 20 years. He was not only completely unable to describe his mother, father, wife or son, but in the two months which followed his wife's death he had not had any dreams about her.

Shortly after his suicide attempt he did have the following dream: he came into his shoemaker's shop and found a fire going in the fireplace. He was surprised because he had not lit it and no one else had a key to the shop. There were many shoes on the bench, and many customers were waiting outside with work to be done.

The fire represented both life and warmth, as his emotional tie to life was largely a tie to work. After he had stopped working, he suffered from acute anxiety attacks, thus repeating a pattern that evolved before his earlier suicide attempt. At that time he had planned to retire, but was advised, in view of his suicidal tendency, to return to work. Following his second attempt at retirement, he again became restless and anxious. His history was that of a man who had filled every free minute with work, taking considerable pride in his steady working record.

What these two patients had in common was the need for work as a relief from anxiety and self-doubt. This pattern was found in many other Swedish patients and often resulted in a rather frenzied kind of overwork. Such patients often attributed their difficulties to overwork, with little realization of the anxiety that was driving them.

Work served as an inordinate source of ego support for Swedish men. Their self-image was focused on their working role, and their self-esteem depended heavily on success at work. Failure in this area made them vulnerable to self-hatred.

Work and performance also served as a major outlet for self-assertion and the discharge of aggression derived from various sources. Aggressiveness and anxiety connected with work was apt to give it a pleasureless, driven quality or, more extremely, led to anxiety and difficulties in performance. Work failure affected not only the man's self-evaluation, but also his usual outlets for the expression of aggression. While the Danish man is vulnerable to the termination of a relationship (a termination that his own dependency may precipitate), the Swede is vulnerable to difficulties related to work or to lack of success. The latter may be caused by his overreliance on work as a source of self-esteem, by aggression connected with his work, and by his rigidly held expectations of work success.

✻   ✻   ✻

The emphasis placed on performance and success by suicidal men by no means precludes the existence of important problems in the relationship between the sexes. It is true that performance failure rather than immediate object loss more commonly precipitates suicide in the male. Nevertheless, the man's attitude toward women plays a crucial role even in relation to his work performance, as the following example may help to demonstrate.

At the age of 38 a man made a suicide attempt in a moment of panic over financial troubles. Following his second marriage about 18 months previously, he made extensive renovations in his grocery store at an expense of 45,000 kroner, and overreached himself financially. During the period which preceded his suicide attempt all of his employees were on vacation, and he and his wife had to work every day. Although they worked together, he concealed his financial troubles from his wife, changing the subject whenever she asked him why he looked so worried. Ascribing the suicide attempt to his need for a protest against too much work, he stressed that his sister and parents had vacations, while he was unable to get away. However, when he was interviewed following a five-day vacation period with his wife, he reported that he had been unable to relax and enjoy her company. He made numerous telephone calls to Stockholm to check on things at the store even though there was no real need to do so.

There was an obsessive, driven quality to his work as was demonstrated by his elaboration of the TAT card which shows men working at a dock. In the story he constructed around this picture, the men were slaves being driven.

The patient proudly described his mother as a leading lady of the town throughout his childhood. She had been engaged in many outside activities as far back as he could remember, but he denied that he had suffered from her absence. Nevertheless, he recalled severe fears of ghosts and darkness as well as fright over the possibility of his mother's death. He characterized her as very ambitious for her children and a perfectionist.

Although he had no conscious complaints about his present wife, his dreams and fantasies revealed a picture of all women and, most importantly, of his wife and mother as demanding, ambitious and overly critical. He drove himself frantically at work, and interpreted his wife's failure to express praise and admiration for him as an indication that she expected too much and was somehow dissatisfied. His suicide attempt was tied up with the intensity of his efforts to succeed at work and with the difficulties encountered in this undertaking. While he kept the difficulties to himself, he became resentful of his wife, because he did not like the position in which he found himself. Unknowingly, he used his work to establish his worth in his own eyes and those of his wife, and he was angry at her because he had to do so. Thus he punished his wife for experiences that had originally occurred with his mother. This combination was rather usual for the Swedish male patient.

The inclination of this patient to withdraw from his wife when he was in difficulty with his work was also usual for the Swedish man. Characteristically, his attitude was: "She can't help me with it, so why tell her about it?" This attitude was maintained without conscious resentment toward the woman in question. A wife was seen as the person to whom a man would come for praise and admiration for successful performance. There were non-suicidal men as well who had histories of withdrawing from, or giving up, their relationship with women when they experienced anxiety as to their ability to cope with their work. One suicidal patient was seen who had delayed his suicidal intentions for many years because he could go to his wife for reassurance. In general, however, men were found to be far less able to utilize women as a source of comfort than are Danes or Americans. Since the woman is seen chiefly as someone for whom to perform well, she is likely to become something of a strain. In Sweden, far more than in Denmark or the United States, men like to relax in each other's company; in the absence of women they feel free to be themselves and enjoy themselves.

The patient's early separation from his mother and his consequent anxiety were also typical of both Swedish suicidal and non-suicidal patients and of non-patients as well. Hence it may be worth while here to give something of the background of this separation and its relation to the Swedish attitude toward performance and competition.

It has been noted earlier that in Denmark it is customary to encourage the child's dependency on his mother and to delay his separation from her. In Sweden the reverse is true. The tendency there is to encourage a very early separation of the child from the mother, and the mother is pleased when she observes evidence of the child's self-sufficiency and independence.

This attitude is not simply that of the working mother, as is true in the United States and Denmark. Swedish mothers do tend to go back to work three months after delivery; many of them admit that they cannot stay home and care for a young child. They know that it might be better for the child, but their own needs are too strong. Often the return to work is rationalized as being due to economic necessity, when it is actually not pressing. The woman simply does not like to care for her child and she prefers to go back to work. Sometimes both husband and wife are more concerned with the things they can buy with their combined earnings than they are with the child's reaction to a separation from the mother. The age range in day-care centers for children whose mothers are working is from three months to six years. "Key children" is the Swedish term for young school children who return to their homes before their parents come back from work. Since the child is too young to be trusted with a loose key, it is tied around his neck.

Even more important is the widespread tendency among those mothers who do stay home, to push their children into an extremely early independence. Some mothers have feelings of guilt over this separation and are inclined to cover it up. However, the emotional need for the separation is very strong.

As one Swedish child psychiatrist stated: "The mothers just don't seem to enjoy their children very much. They don't get the same pleasure from their children—whether caring for them or playing with them—that you see in Danish and American mothers."

Early separation becomes the source of a great deal of anxiety and resentment, although there is usually no physical neglect and the child knows no other pattern. Finding no justification for being angry with the mother, most Swedish males deny that they were hurt. The average patient will simply say that he had the nicest mother in the world—and then try to change the subject. He has long since learned to consider his dependency needs unacceptable. He denies their existence and masks them behind an apparent self-reliance.

Childhood phobias, particularly fears of darkness and thunder, appeared frequently in the histories of both Swedish patients and non-patients. Also common were fears of losing the mother through death. Such fears were a mixture of separation anxiety and anger and often presented the first clue to disturbance in the mother-child relationship. Sleeping difficulties of the young child, pointing to a similar type of anxiety, are one of the main reasons why Swedish mothers with young children seek psychiatric help.

The tendency to separate young children from the mother applies to both sexes. Between the ages of 5 and 10, however, the boy is away from the house and out on his own more than the girl. He can play as he wants to and is free from any household chores and responsibilities. The little girl, on the other hand, has a fair number of household duties and learns to be competent in them. Both the girl and her mother tend to cater to the boy in the family, if there is one. In this process, while girls may become envious of the boys' freedom, they reap some advantage from greater contact with their mothers. A girl's self-confidence is as likely as that of a boy to be impaired by early separation from the mother although her later experiences (ages 5-10) may give her the feeling of being more competent than the boy.

The histories of many suicidal patients, non-suicidal patients and non-patients in Sweden contain a reference to the fact that in their early childhood they were reared for long periods by someone other than the mother. These were not children born illegitimately but children whose mothers found it convenient for various reasons to have the child raised by someone else, often the child's grandmother. Even this arrangement seemed to stem from the same general disturbance in the mother-child relationship.

Here, too, many male suicidal patients handled their response to the situation by means of denial. One man had been in day nurseries from the age of two. When he was six years old and his mother remarried, he was turned over to his grandmother. He was conscious of no grievance against his mother and declared that they had been good friends to this day. He was sure that he had enjoyed his experience in the day nursery. At the same time, however, his earliest and most vivid childhood memory was that of crying in terror as his mother left him in the nursery. In his current life he was completely exploitative in his relations with women.

As to the origin of the previously mentioned competitiveness and performance concern, it should be noted that from the child's earliest age Swedish parents are more interested in his performance and how he compares with other children than are Danish parents. The child learns to use his performance to bolster his self-esteem and to appear more lovable in the eyes of his parents.

At the age of about ten, a shift takes place in what is expected of Swedish boys and girls. The boy, who has been playing as he pleases, experiences a new and intense interest on the part of his family in his performance, particularly at school. He can win parental approval and admiration with success, and is expected to do so, or he may cause consternation by his failure. The school competition for boys who want to go on with their education, or whose parents want them to, is a fierce one. The number of places available for higher education is limited, and the school system is based on merit. Many educated Swedes speak with intense feelings of the toil that took place before they completed the *student examen* necessary for their advanced education. Work and performance become the natural means to repair whatever damage to self-esteem has been caused by early separation, and to win maternal admiration and attention. The boy whose self-esteem has not been too severely damaged by early separation and whose aggression has not been too strongly curbed, may be able to go through this stage of transition successfully and can become an extremely effective and productive person. However, the task required of him is by no means an easy one.

* * *

In order to understand the group of female suicidal patients and their motivations for suicide, it may be helpful to refer to that Swedish woman whose case was used as an illustration in the chapter on the psychodynamics of suicide. The following details of her history are of interest here.

At the age of 44, one year after the breakup of her marriage, the patient made a serious suicide attempt with 30 sleeping pills. She had married her husband who was five years her senior when she was 22 years old after having known him for three years. From the beginning of their relationship he was "nervous, jealous and domineering." He frequently accused her without justification of "having something to do with other men." During the first nine years of their marriage he had often been away from home since he was the traveling representative of a business firm. He received many letters from other women, but she claimed to have always accepted his explanation that the letters came "from friends." Much later she admitted that in some way she had realized that he was unfaithful to her. However, she had either repressed this knowledge or reassured herself by minimizing the importance of these affairs.

For the past few years her husband had a steady affair with a 33 year old divorced woman who had an 11 year old child. Although he apparently did not wish to leave the patient and their two children, a boy of 19 and a girl of 15, she forced the issue by barging in on him in the other woman's apartment. He was furious and openly moved in with this woman. A few months later the patient tried to console herself with a younger man at her office, but the relationship gave her no satisfaction.

The patient's explanation following her suicide attempt was that she had failed as a woman and that her husband as well as her children would be better off if she were dead. In her latest suicide attempt the patient had taken over 30 sleeping pills, but was fortunately discovered by a friend in time. Ten days earlier she had made another suicide attempt: she went out to a lake with the intention of drowning herself. However, she changed her mind, went home and took 15 sleeping pills there.

She woke up 36 hours later and recalled the following dream: she saw a cap belonging to her husband's father floating on the sea, and realized that he had drowned. He was a sea captain and very much like her husband—extremely domineering, critical and difficult to get along with. The two men did not like each other. In fact, her husband had often said that he would be indifferent to his father's death. At first she discussed the dream in terms of her own martyred role, but eventually she showed her desire to strike back at her husband. She spoke vindictively of the problems with the children that her death would cause him. She feared that her suicide might be futile because he would not care. In her dream, he was to be drowned and she would be indifferent. On the whole, she was a woman who was ineffectual in expressing both anger and self-assertion, and she could not even successfully fight for her children.

The patient had been the middle child between an older and a younger brother. Her mother "never had time for her" and had constantly and unfairly criticized whatever she did. By contrast, she had first been fond of her father, but later lost respect for him because he let her mother rule the family. While her mother was always sick, complaining and unkind, her father was calm, quiet and occasionally affectionate.

By and large, the patient's husband had taken over her mother's role. He was critical of what she did around the house, how she behaved with people, etc. She thought that she had been too submissive and had never been able to be angry, probably because she was afraid of her husband's anger. Her own daughter had lost respect for her because of this weakness.

Her suicidal psychodynamics were typical of one main group of female patients, whose suicide attempts were tied up with frustrated anger over male infidelity or abandonment. It was repeated infidelity on the part of a man that frequently precipitated such suicide attempts. While these women sometimes had extramarital affairs themselves, they initiated them in retaliation for male infidelity and neglect. For the woman, such a retaliatory act failed to serve as an adequate countermeasure.

The childhood histories of these women were remarkably similar. They described their mothers as demanding, critical and unloving. Their self-confidence was impaired, with self-assertion and initiative crushed at an early age. When they were ready to form relationships with men, they merely changed to receiving abuse from their husbands instead of their mothers. Criticism, neglect and infidelity were their lot in marriage; and suicide was their way of trying to strike back.

One such suicidal woman was 43 years old and had three children, aged 13, 15 and 22. She had been divorced three times from husbands who had been unfaithful. Her suicide attempt was triggered by the possibility of a breakup with her current boyfriend. She had grown up in a home where her parents were unhappy and never affectionate with either each other or the children. Her father was described as a brutal alcoholic who "hated us all." Her mother seemed to have been fond only of the patient's eldest brother, a child fathered by another man prior to her marriage to the patient's father. Even as a young child the patient was kept occupied by her mother with work to be done around the house. She was rarely permitted to be out playing with the other children.

During the course of the interviews she had the following dream: her boyfriend left her because she had not cleaned up her apartment. She was unhappy in the dream and felt he did not have sufficient reason for deserting her.

The day before she had the dream was her first day on a new job, and she came home too tired to do her housework. Following a telephone conversation with her boyfriend, she was disappointed because he had given her little encouragement or reassurance with regard to her job. He intended to go to work in another town, and while he had discussed the possibility of her joining him there, her feeling was that he neither meant what he said nor really wanted her to join him. Her dream imagery indicated how rooted she was in her childhood view of the world. She always was the "bad little girl" who did not do her chores well enough, and rejection was her punishment.

In this patient as well as in many other suicidal women, it was relatively easy to discern the disturbance in the child-mother relationship, since it was not as disguised and hidden as it was in the men. The women were at least able to express some bitterness over what they regarded as maternal rejection in childhood.

While the childhood deprivations of these women were severe, their histories reflected certain tendencies seen in the non-suicidal female patients and non-patient nurses as well. As stated before, early separation from the mother applies to both sexes, although many boys enjoy freedom from the chores required of the girls. Around the age of ten, when increasing interest is shown in the performance of boys, girls may experience the disappointment of seeing less emphasis placed on their achievements. A girl's school failure is not the same catastrophe as is that of her brother, and her good marks receive less admiration. Her household chores are taken for granted, although she may still attempt to build self-esteem and control aggression by obediently performing these duties. In so doing, she may go on to become a meticulous housewife—often too meticulous for her husband's taste.* In girls who follow this course as well as in those who rebel against it, the idea of cleanliness and orderliness being psychologically equated with goodness and obedience remains strongly ingrained.

In her teens the girl's interest is expected to center around her popularity with boys, and her self-esteem depends on her success with them. Her self-confidence, if already impaired, is not helped by the boy's coolness. It is ironic that in a country known for the beauty of its women, these same women are rather insecure about their attractiveness. Some girls accept successful work or a career as their goals, although too much achievement or success tends to be regarded as unfeminine. Hence they are likely to have inhibitions about success or doing their best, simply because they are afraid of losing their femininity and their chances of being happy with men. Even those women who strive hard for success in a career or at work have less rigid standards for themselves and their performance than have the men. The success driven women were not found among the Swedish suicidal patients; they were observed as patients with other problems, as the wives of suicidal men, or among the nurses that were studied.

---

* The woman devotes more effort and concern to the neatness, cleanliness and quality of the dress of her child than is usual in the United States or in the rest of Scandinavia.

Apparently the toilet training of the Swedish child takes place earlier and in a shorter period than in our children. This fact may be correlated as much with the mother's interest in an independently functioning child as with her interest in cleanliness and orderliness. There is a great deal of Swedish humor centering around bowel and bladder functions and the passing of flatus. These jokes generally serve to deflate or humiliate someone through humorously calling attention to his natural functions.

The pattern of female suicide, precipitated either by repeated male infidelity or by total abandonment, is obviously not restricted to Sweden. However, when the Swedish girl forms a love relationship on which her self-esteem is supposed to rest, she is hampered by those traumatic childhood experiences connected with an early separation from her mother. Moreover, her capacities for self-assertion and aggression may have been further impaired by certain parental attitudes (which will be discussed later) toward such behavior. Of course, the weaknesses in self-assertion, aggression and self-esteem are not very helpful in holding the man, nor are the man's attitudes toward women, based on his own childhood experiences, in her favor. If infidelity or abandonment occurs, the woman often lacks those adaptive tools which she would need to cope with the situation. The whole combination of circumstances leads to more disappointed women, more impotent rage and self-hatred, and a somewhat greater number of female suicides than are seen in the United States.*

Even on the popular level the nature of the trouble is somehow recognized. There are standard jokes about the love and attention that the Swedish man bestows upon his car, and his lack of love and attention for his wife. There is the popular type of cartoon that depicts a young, attractive, well-built Swedish girl sitting in a restaurant and being ignored by her boyfriend who is busily reading the sports pages in a newspaper. The magazine stories for women are particularly interesting in this regard, one of their main themes being as follows: a woman, single or married, not too confident and only moderately attractive, loses her man, usually to a sexually more seductive woman. Sometimes the man just disappears after a misunderstanding. Apparently such stories serve as an outlet for the woman's disappointment and pain and, to a lesser degree, her anger. The stories usually have wishful and unreal endings, in which the man comes back suddenly, sometimes years later, and finally aware of the more enduring virtues of the deserted woman. If he disappeared rather

---

* The Swedish female suicide rate of approximately 7.5/100,000 is 1½ times higher than the U.S. female rate of 5, and three times the Norwegian female rate of 2.5. However, the rate for Swedish women is not nearly so striking when one considers that the Danish female rate of close to 15/100,000 is almost twice the Swedish rate, three times the U.S. rate and five times the Norwegian female rate.

than left for another woman, it was in order to make his fortune so that he could come home successful and marry his sweetheart. The ending is not particularly relevant, but the story itself seems to appeal to many women who have undergone rejection and disappointment in their experiences with men.

*   *   *

In the other main group of female suicidal patients, the relationship with the mother was found to be even more significant. These women remained actively tied to their mothers, and their emotional relationships with men were at best of secondary importance.

One 25 year old girl had made a suicide attempt at the age of 24 by turning on the gas in her parents' summer home and then taking sleeping pills. Earlier attempts had been made at the age of 17 by cutting her wrists and at the age of 21 by turning on the gas. Although her most recent attempt had taken place one year previously, she appeared acutely suicidal during the time I was seeing her. In fact, she did kill herself by jumping from a building eight months later.

The patient was a tall, dark-haired, thin girl who shook from anxiety during her first three interviews. Lacking emotional control, she rapidly changed from tears to fury during our talks. Any mention of her mother sufficed to produce rage almost immediately.

According to the patient's story, her mother still regulated her life and told her what to do. "She was always opposed to my having fun and whatever I did was wrong." In particular, the patient complained that her mother was opposed to all of her boy-friends, and the patient often felt compelled to listen to her advice about them.

Throughout her childhood, her mother was out evenings with other men, while her father was out with his own friends. In the beginning her mother had made an effort to keep her infidelity a secret. In recent years, however, one man came openly to the house and her father had to put up with the situation. When the patient herself was old enough to go out with men, she began getting revenge on her mother. At the age of 17 she became pregnant. Apparently her first suicide attempt was motivated by this pregnancy and was partially designed to obtain a psychiatric abortion.

During her college years the patient had an affair with a student who was very fond of her. Shortly before graduation she was again pregnant, but refused to get married. She planned to have the baby and live with her parents in their summer villa, while the boy wanted to marry her, have the baby and move into their own apartment. Her mother was opposed to her marriage, the baby, and their moving into the summer villa, and her view prevailed. Since the patient felt unable to oppose her mother, she permitted her to help in obtaining an abortion. Several months later in an acute psychotic depression she heard voices reproaching her for having had the abortion.

After her boyfriend had married someone else, she became involved with, and eventually engaged to, another boy. Once again shying away from marriage, she made her third suicidal attempt because she was dissatisfied with this relationship and could not forget her former boyfriend. She saw this boy occasionally and hoped that his marriage might come to an end so that she could have him. Under pressure she admitted that even if he became available, she would probably not marry him. One dream during her observational period in the hospital was revealing with regard to her suicidal motivation.

Some little children were drowning. She wanted to save them. A girl whom she had known as a child attempted to prevent her from rescuing them. She had her hands on this girl's throat and intended to choke her when she woke up.

In the group of children who were drowning, the patient knew only herself. The other person in the dream was a girl against whom she had never been able to defend herself. "This girl would always criticize my appearance and all I did—she was as bad as my mother." In a paranoid, dependent, enraged way she was tied to her mother, with suicide being the only outlet for her murderous feelings.

What this patient had in common with several others was a history of maternal separation and abandonment followed by what they regarded as too much maternal control when they were older. Their mothers were hated by them, because they controlled them and interfered with their lives. They were hardly aware of how dependent they were and how much they needed and invited this control. They were also unaware of the even more important abandonment trauma that created their need for so much control. These girls were grossly paranoid, and their anger spilled over toward everyone. However, several women who earlier in life had been able to repress this anger later developed more classical paranoid symptoms—their delusions centering around their guilt over anger toward their mothers.

One married woman in this group was 50 years old when she developed many paranoid ideas prior to her suicide attempt. She thought that her neighbors were watching her and saying bad things about her, for instance, that she did not clean her house well and spent too much time caring for her flower garden instead. When she was out shopping, she had the idea that people in the stores might accuse her of having stolen something, although she had never done anything like that and was unaware of any desire to do so. She was afraid that neighbors might ask the government authorities to take her 14 year old daughter (she also has a son aged 17) away from her because she had been a bad mother. She was a shy woman and had always been afraid of her neighbors, but she had never before expressed overt paranoid ideas about them.

The patient's symptoms began soon after her father's death one year previously. She thought that she should give her ill mother more help and felt guilty over her unwillingness to do so. A few times she had prepared food for her mother, but felt she should also be helping her more around the house.

The patient grew up in a family that was always on the edge of poverty. Her father was a truck loader and described as an outgoing man who liked company. However, he drank a lot and was always in debt, while her mother liked to be by herself and was often tired and depressed. She had threatened twice to drown herself when the patient was a young girl, and each time was persuaded by the patient and her older sister to come home. Her mother loved to read, and the patient took after her in this respect. She also recalled much childhood anxiety about her desire to do well in school. As a child she was terrified by thunder and was very much afraid of the dark.

When the patient was 18 years old, her mother bought a fruit store which the patient and her sister were to help manage.

Because of heavy debts, her mother and sister abandoned the store. The patient stayed on until she was 27 years old to repay her mother's debts, and had many quarrels with her mother during this period. She recalled that coming home from work she would find that her mother had been in bed all day. The house was sloppy, supper was not ready, and the dishes had not been done.

The patient was 26 when she married. Her husband sold hardware and was described by her as more social and less intellectual than she. While she considered herself a stronger person than her husband, she was aware of no serious problems either with him or her two children. Later on it became clear that although she may have had few problems with her husband and children, there also was a limited degree of emotional involvement with them. Her most intense feelings and emotions went into the relationship with her mother.

She became tearful in telling that she had been sick in the hospital for a month after the birth of her daughter and that neither parent had come to visit her. Eight years prior to her current difficulties her parents had decided to build a house, although she and her husband had tried to dissuade them because of the debts to be incurred. Following her father's death, there arose the question of what to do with the house. Neither she and her husband nor her sister and her husband were willing to pay the debt. She wanted her mother to sell the house and go into a home for the aged. She cried again while saying that her mother would miss the flower garden. Both she and her mother loved to care for flowers.

Several nights after her admission to the hospital, the patient had the following dream: an old woman was leaving the hospital, dressed in a drab beige outfit. She wished to give the woman a new red outfit and looked for one that she had sewn for her daughter. The older woman leaving the hospital was both she and her mother. The drabness of the mother's outfit suggested her current drab existence. The red outfit was one that she had actually given to her daughter.

In taking something from her daughter and giving it to her mother, she revealed the fear that she had been a bad mother to her daughter. Her desire to win her mother's favor had always come first and reduced her ability to give real affection to her daughter. When she was younger, she had hoped through self-sacrifice to gain her mother's affection. She had little hope now of receiving anything from her mother. To the contrary, she was faced with having to be a mother to her mother. In the dream she wanted to hold on to the ingratiating attitude toward her mother, characteristic of her earlier years. However, this adaptive move was of little use at present and was failing her. Since her angry feelings toward her mother were too dangerous to face, she defended herself against them with her paranoid symptoms.

❖   ❖   ❖

The Swedish woman's relations with her children played a less significant role in influencing her decision regarding suicide than was true for women in the United States or Denmark. Women who are angry at having to care for children and feel guilty over this anger or at least guilty over abandoning their children through suicide are a common part of the suicidal problem in Denmark, the United States and, as we shall see later, in Norway. However, the Swedish women who had little feeling for their children appeared less tortured by this lack of feeling than American or Danish mothers would be in a comparable situation. Such a motive for suicide did not occur in the Swedish group; even in the woman's dreams of suicide her children were not significant. On the other hand, concern with the consequences of suicide on surviving children is probably less of a preventive factor on female suicide in Sweden than it is for women in other countries.

One particular sexual problem may throw further light on the disturbance in the mother-child relationship in Sweden. Several Swedish psychiatrists and psychoanalysts emphasized that women frequently withdraw sexually from their husbands after the birth of a child. This is not simply a case of the woman wanting a child and of the man being against it. In such a situation she would be expected to be more emotionally involved with the child. Nor is the withdrawal initiated by the man.

The birth of a child often creates a situation that reveals the underlying stresses between men and women. Mention was previously made of the common observation of Danish analysts that impotence in the man follows the birth of the child, stemming from his feeling of having been displaced. There is a fair probability that the Swedish woman's sexual withdrawal is explained by anger toward the man because of the child. One of her common complaints about the husband is what is called "his irresponsibility." By this she means his freedom to come and go as he pleases, while she is expected not only to work, but also to care for her household and children in the evening. In this respect the wife's envy of the man is not unlike the young girl's previously noted envy of the boy's freedom to play as he pleases. Likewise her feeling of greater competence and responsibility is similar to the young girl's attitude toward the boy. The arrival of a child may aggravate this envy and resentment of the man's freedom, forcing the woman into a reluctant acceptance of the female role. Moreover, this reaction would be consistent with the previously described encouragement of the child's independence and his separation from the mother. Women who themselves have experienced such an early separation are often unable emotionally to treat their children differently, even if they would like them to have a more secure childhood.

Swedish magazines reflect the mother-child situation in a characteristic way. While in American and Danish magazines children are running all over the pages, their absence is conspicuous in the Swedish stories. If they exist, they have no character or personality, and their relations with their mothers are completely in the background. Even more important is the fact that they are not prime factors in the woman's considerations or in her deliberations about her problems. Interestingly, in the Danish stories it is often the woman's maternal qualities, with a child of a prior marriage or with a waif that she has found, which induce the man to want her.

❊   ❊   ❊

One of the most common marital complaints in Sweden concerns difficulty in reaching the marital partner emotionally, and it is usually the woman who makes this complaint about the man. There is an apt Swedish idiom, *tiga ihjäl,* meaning—to kill somebody through silence. This tendency to control anger through detachment apparently results in a general dampening of affectivity and interferes with the ability to sustain interest in a marital relationship. As a rule, this attitude is more strongly expressed in the man than in the woman.

In a mild form such detachment is partly under the individual's control and can be used deliberately. One patient, for example, asked his wife in a suicide note to forgive his "pretended insensitivity." The most exaggerated detachment was seen in schizophrenics and served to hide both anxiety regarding ego collapse and paranoid destructiveness.

One 31 year old married suicidal patient supplied little information in his first sessions, except for the facts that he was anxious, felt slightly depressed and considered himself a failure at work. The extent of his detachment was the most striking feature. His suicide note to his wife was filled with phrases such as "all my life I've been hiding behind a shell" and "a wall has been built up around me."

Eventually he related that his wife had confessed infidelity a few years previously. Although he wanted to be "reasonable" and had forgiven her, he would think of it during sexual intercourse, become enraged and hit her. His anger in retelling this episode pushed aside his detachment for a while, as was shown by a whole series of dreams. In one of them he was in a room and the ceiling caved in. In another he was in quicksand, and in a third he was in a tunnel which collapsed. Finally he had a dream in which "the ground split" and he "fell in." All the dreams reflected the imminent danger of ego collapse that threatened him.

The patient's wife blamed his aloofness and detachment for her infidelity. She spoke of his tendency to withdraw from her when he had trouble at work or when there was some trouble between them. She preferred to have difficulties aired and finished, while he would become silent and stay angry for a long time. Complaints of this kind, with the man withdrawing when angry or seeking an outlet for his anger in some activity away from home, ranging from intensified work to alcoholism, were again and again expressed by women whose husbands were much better integrated than this patient. When his wife had to be interviewed a full hour, he confessed that he had to control the urge to punch me in jealous rage. However, this was the beginning of an improved emotional contact between us.

Some kind of provocation such as the one that occurred accidentally with this last patient was often necessary for penetrating this detachment. Another patient was not only detached, but intent on being a "good boy" during the initial interviews. His entire personality structure served the purpose of keeping his anger under control, and enormous self-hatred ensued. This self-hatred centered around his big nose, on which he blamed everything, from his shyness to his potency difficulties, and he hoped to talk the hospital physicians into a plastic operation. When in one session he was questioned about the fact that he had arranged for his mother to find his body after his suicide attempt, he denied that he had wanted to hurt her with this attempt.

That night he dreamt that he was forced by a man into a fight. When he took his coat off, the man began to hit him with a stick. In self-defense he threw the man into a pool, and the man was drowned. The patient tried to save the man by extending a stick into the water, but the man refused to save himself in order to make the patient feel guilty. He then dreamt of a woman who was lying on the floor with a bloody face.

Following the interview with me, the patient was disturbed by the idea that he might have wished to hurt his mother. He took this thought as an accusation and considered it unfair. In his dream, apart from retaliating for this unfairness, he said to me in effect: "You are the sort of person who would kill himself to hurt someone, not me." He identified the woman in the second part of the dream as representing both himself and his mother, who also had a big nose. His nose seemed to be associated with everything that was bad and aggressive about him. Its removal would be a partial suicide and a partial castration for him and, like suicide itself, was regarded as a destructive act aimed at his mother as well as himself.

This patient resembled some of the previously discussed paranoid female patients whose suicide attempt represented psychodynamically a murderous attack on their mothers. However, he was more paranoid toward the world and repressed his anger toward his mother—a modification observed particularly in male patients.

One 31 year old, well built, handsome man was timid, polite and deferential, almost to the point of servility. His life story was a mixture of shyness and apathy characterized by chronic feelings of emotional deadness. Every few years this state was interrupted by anxiety attacks during which he was unable to function. His anxiety could be triggered by mounting pressure in various areas, either by a woman or at work. In a typical dream indicative of his anxiety about ego disintegration, he was in a wooded area when a strong wind uprooted all the bushes and trees. Holding on to one tree after another, he finally was pushed by the wind into a lake and under the water.

The patient was preoccupied with religious problems. He suspected that his suicide attempt was foolish, since life after death would probably be a continuation of the pleasureless, apathetic deadness that he had always known.

His feeling of emotional deadness, his view of life as a pleasureless chore, and his conception of an afterlife as a continuation of that chore were themes that recurred in many Swedish patients and had a uniquely Swedish quality. His idea of an afterlife contained no special punishment; none was needed, since continuation would be punishment enough.

In an earlier chapter emphasis was placed on the manner in which strong feelings of detachment, repressed aggression and dampened affectivity can be psychologically perceived as a kind of emotional dying or death. It was noted that such deadness is experienced as extremely torturous and that suicide is regarded as the execution of something that has already happened. Individuals with such feelings in any culture are more likely to take their lives than almost any other group of patients. In varying intensity this syndrome was found to be characteristic of the Swedish patients.

The Swedish patients made greater efforts to conceal or minimize their suicide attempts than did the Danes, reflecting the greater shame they attached to suicide. They frequently expressed the feeling that suicide was cowardly and an act of weakness and failure, an attitude that was consistent with the Swede's concern with his performance. Dread of the reaction of family members to their suicide attempt played an important role in their shame, while shame derived from religious principles was of little significance.

About one-half of the Swedish patients stressed that they believed in God, but only 50 per cent of these thought that there was an afterlife. Some of the believers in God denied their belief at first, but expressed it later, indicating that they had been ashamed and did not want to be ridiculed. It seemed to be more shameful to believe than not to believe. The proportion of believers was slightly in excess of 50 per cent if the question was formulated somewhat as follows: "Do you believe that there is anything behind everything that happens in the world and that there is some purpose or intention to life?" Many of those believing in an afterlife considered it unlikely that persons killing themselves would attain it. (This opinion contrasted with that of Danish suicidal patients believing in an afterlife. They expected to be forgiven for their suicide and looked forward to being happy in an afterlife.) Placing a high value on rationality, the Swedes try to suppress as well as repress the irrational, the mystical and the magical in their character.

✣   ✣   ✣

Differences in the development of male and female affectivity can also be traced to childhood. Many observations made in the past few decades have indicated that while the potential for affectivity is inborn, the actual capacity for love and tenderness is developed in the early years of life, primarily in the mother-child relationship. The early separation of mother and child and the relatively little pleasure derived by the Swedish mother from contact with her young child are likely to contribute greatly to the widespread affectivity problems seen in Sweden.

However, there are other contributing factors. The Swedish child, especially the boy, is taught not to show too much feeling. Much emphasis is placed on the child's ability to be reasonable and unemotional even in disturbing situations. To be *tyst och lugn*, that is, quiet and calm, is something of a Swedish ideal, particularly for the boy and the adult man.

Girls can cry, boys should not. Neither boys nor girls are allowed to express anger toward parents and siblings as openly as are American children. Within the house, however, little girls are permitted to have a somewhat undirected temper tantrum that will be tolerated as "hysterical" or "feminine." A boy's expression of anger would be considered uncontrolled and unmanly, although the freedom enjoyed by him gives him at least one advantage over the Danish boy. He is able to slam the door, to go out and play, and to express his anger in some form of disobedience. He thereby learns to take his anger away from the family and to act it out. If, as a husband, he continues this pattern, his conduct is at least consistent.

It is also consistent with such a behavior pattern that the Swedish young man tends to regard all emotion as feminine. The affectivity difficulties that are to play such an important role in the relations between the sexes are already evident by adolescence. While Swedish teenagers are somewhat freer sexually than are most teenage groups in the United States, the boy's coolness makes it necessary for the girl to take more initiative with him than an American girl has to take. Late teenagers are not compelled to cover up their sexual activities to the same extent as is the rule for the American teenager, and the parents make a great effort to be "reasonable."* However, a fair amount of the sexual contact between teenagers is not simply a matter of less restriction or prohibition. Instead, sex is used by boys and girls who have difficulties with their affectivity, for the purpose of trying to make some kind of contact.

As an adult, the Swedish man is likely to feel that strong emotions in his wife and his expected responses pose something of a threat or even an attack. One Swedish psychoanalyst put it rather well by saying that the Swedish woman is happiest who can make the transition from wanting emotional evidence from the man, to settling for loyalty and consideration as signs of his affection.

The man is also likely to keep aloof from close emotional contact with his children, thereby affecting their image of him. While the Swedish father is popularly considered to rule the family, his remoteness tends to modify the actual situation. For

---

* The attitude of Swedish parents toward sexual activity displayed by their young children is to prohibit it and to deny its existence at the same time, as is done by American and Danish parents. There is a difference in that young children are not educated to feel the same degree of shame with regard to bodily exposure as children in the United States are. At the age of five or six, children can be seen swimming undressed at the public beaches, while this custom is generally stopped several years earlier in the United States. Thus the adult, too, is not likely to experience the same degree of pain or panic that is seen here if he or she is observed undressed.

example, children will observe how the mother caters to the father and gives in to him in open conflict. At the same time, however, she will manage some of the most important family affairs by herself, without the necessity of paternal participation. In any case, one-half of the patients and non-patients in the present study considered their mothers to have been the stronger and more effective force in their families.

The relationship between lack of contact and underlying anger is clearly expressed in the cartoons of the famous Swedish humorist and caricaturist, Albert Engström. Over and over in his cartoons, lack of contact serves as a vehicle for the discharge of aggression. The judge asks the man in court why he beat up so many policemen. The man replies that if he had concentrated all those blows on one policeman he would have hurt him too badly.

Probably the finest examples and most graphic descriptions of aggressiveness and detachment and their meaning in the Swedish character can be found in the writing of the Nobel Prize laureate, Pär Lagerkvist[1]. Barabbas is the epitomy of the man who goes through life as an observer rather than a participant. His affectivity is slightly stimulated by alcohol, and his rage is released by injustice—first by the murder of the hare-lipped girl and finally by his misunderstanding of the Christian cause. He contemplates a martyred religious view of life, but never successfully or convincingly. For the most part he is detached, although preoccupation with death never leaves him. At the end: "Death! He always had that inside him, he had had that inside him as long as he had lived. It hunted him inside himself, in the dark mole's passages of his mind, and filled him with its terror."

The Dwarf is the personification of aggression, evil, avarice and destructiveness. At the end of the book, when he is locked up by the prince in a dungeon but knows that the prince will call on him again, he is clearly depicted as being more than the prince's tool: he is the hidden part of the prince's personality. One might take a slight license with the two books to say that behind the detachment of a Barabbas lies the need to control the aggression of the Dwarf.

In *The Eternal Smile, Guest of Reality, The Hangman* and his shorter stories and poems, Lagerkvist equates life with death, based on the inability to love or to feel. The "living dead" come to life when attacked—being permitted then to release their rage. In this sense the vicious or antisocial are more alive than others, and those who see society as the enemy are at least protected from such feelings of deadness. Without an enemy there is only death in life, psychologically precipitated by strangulated rage and strangulated affectivity. Nor is Lagerkvist alone in Swedish literature in this preoccupation with death. Lagerkvist, Sjöberg, Hallström, Dagerman and a host of other Swedish authors have perhaps produced the world's most prolific and sensitive literature on death.[2]

Americans who, to their own loss, are unfamiliar with Lagerkvist's work, may see this combination of detachment and destructiveness in the films of Ingmar Bergman. Destructiveness is more conspicuous there, but the knight in *The Seventh Seal* and the professor in *Wild Strawberries* are excellent examples of the type of detachment that has been described here.

In a minor key, Swedish literary journals are filled with discussions of whether or not life is boring in Sweden. Foreigners complaining about Stockholm in this manner may largely refer to the fact that the city is not a playground, which is probably a compliment rather than an insult. However, when such a complaint is made by Swedes, it has to be taken more seriously. The usual ascription of *tråkighet* (boredom) to external conditions seems incorrect. Boredom is more likely a sign of internal affective difficulties and the consequent diminished capacity for enjoying life, especially in persons who suffer most from it. Some of the Swedes' liking for the Danes and the people of southern Europe stems from their appreciation of the greater emotional freedom displayed by these people, at least in initial contacts.

        ✿   ✿   ✿

Of the social and psychological constellations described, it seems to be the early separation of the child, the relationship between the sexes, the control of aggression and its effect on affectivity, and the attitudes toward competition and performance which are of the greatest significance in determining Swedish life and psychosocial character. Stockholmers, or certainly their parents, come from all parts of Sweden, and one cannot work with patients in that city without observing some of the variations which prevail in different parts of the country. For example, competitiveness among the men is greater in Stockholm than in the rural areas, where control of affectivity is particularly pronounced. However, this study aims at defining the characteristics distinguishing Sweden, especially as compared to the United States and Denmark (and later Norway), rather than those differentiating the Swedes. A comprehensive study of the variations in character and family patterns within the country should be undertaken as a separate project. It would probably prove to be of great value to Swedish psychiatry.

Mention may be made in this connection of one patient who did not at all fit into the patterns described here. He was a 48 year old man who was depressed rather than anxious. He was mourning the loss of a slightly older woman with whom he had had a lengthy affair (four years) until she rejected him about eight months earlier. Working as an elevator operator, he had been reasonably content with his economic situation and expected that as long as he could manage financially without too much difficulty he would be satisfied. His relations with his most recent girlfriend, as well as with his wife who had died 20 years earlier, and with his mother and sister had been characterized by marked dependency upon them. Following the death of his wife he went home to live with his mother and sister, and until recently he had always managed to have a woman to take care of him. At the time when he lost his girlfriend, however, all the female members of his own family had died, and he doubted that he could find another woman to replace her. His story was unique for a Swedish suicidal patient, but had been common in Denmark. He came closer than any other Swedish patient to fitting the classical description of a "mama's boy," although his dependency demands were less openly expressed than those of Danish patients. He had not been separated from his mother at an early age. Instead, he had a history that was characteristically Danish in that his mother had actually encouraged him to remain dependent upon her as long as possible.

The mother's discipline had also been of the Danish type and created feelings of guilt in him whenever he hurt her. He definitely believed that after his death he would be reunited with both his wife and his mother—an idea more common among Danish than Swedish patients. What remains to be added is that it was only ten years earlier that he had come from Visby on the island of Gotland. For various reasons the patterns of life on this island, like some other areas in southern Sweden, resemble the Danish patterns much more closely than do those of most of the Swedish mainland.

❋   ❋   ❋

How do the patterns that have been discussed fit together to produce the Swedish suicide rate?

The child's early separation from the mother stimulates anger and at the same time deflates self-esteem. The control over anger and other strong affects requires that anger be handled with a great deal of detachment. Few combinations provide such fertile soil for suicide as affective deadening combined with, and based on, the need to control aggression. In the male, competitive performance is an acceptable salve for his self-esteem and may serve as an outlet for his aggression if he can so channel it. Because of rigid expectations for his own performance, however, the man becomes vulnerable to self-hatred and suicide if he fails in this area.

In the female, greater affectivity serves as a protective device. Although likewise damaged by early separation from the mother, her self-esteem can be restored by a stable relationship with a man if properly handled. However, her low self-esteem is not particularly helpful in arousing and sustaining the man's interest in her. Male attitudes toward women tend to aggravate the situation still further. Similar difficulties in dealing with aggression may be the woman's undoing if her relationship with the man develops poorly.

In both male and female cases, whenever the injury from the maternal relationship is more severe or the reaction to it more profound, an active paranoid attachment to the mother may become more important than any tie to work or to the opposite sex. In such circumstances suicide often represents a destructive act aimed at both the patient and his mother.

✿   ✿   ✿

Sweden's social,[3] economic[4] and cultural progress in this century has been a remarkable story, which has led to much envy, resentment or admiration in the rest of Scandinavia. Her standard of living is higher than that of any other European country, and may be behind only those of the United States and Canada. Even this last difference may be more apparent than real, because it has been more difficult in Sweden than in the United States to accumulate great wealth. On the other hand, there also is less poverty than we have here, and while it may not be possible for the average citizen to become wealthy, the country as a whole is.

Many of Sweden's social, economic and welfare achievements are widely known and well documented. Equally remarkable for a country with only seven million inhabitants is the fact that Swedish literature of the past 80 years is fully comparable to that of any other country in the world during the same period.[5] It is only the limited use of the Swedish language throughout the world that has prevented Swedish literature from becoming more popular.

Despite her political neutralism, Sweden is thoroughly Western in her values.[6] What is regarded as particularly Western—the importance of the individual, his personal freedom, and the feeling that no one is expendable– is based on values that are as strong in Sweden as in any other country in the West. If, for example, the Swedes are building more and more nursery day-care centers for the children of working mothers, they are not motivated by the idea that by separating mother and child they may be able to raise a better state citizen. Instead, this is a case of the Swedish government responding to the needs and pressures of the working mothers, who after childbirth want to return to work as soon as possible. Books and articles maintaining that freedom for women includes freedom from having to raise one's own children are very popular in Sweden.[7]

Of course, democratic motivation provides no protection from the harmful consequences of a given social institution. In Sweden as well as in the United States, Denmark or any other country, one questions whether it would be possible to maintain the country's achievements at a lower psychosocial cost. The writer would like to think so. It is only as countries begin to solve their economic problems reasonably well that they are in a position to investigate their social institutions and national adaptive patterns. From this standpoint, Sweden is in a better position than most countries to undertake such investigation.

CHAPTER VI

Suicide in Norway

WHY ARE THE NORWEGIANS less prone to suicide than the Danes and the Swedes? By its negative formulation, the question suggests that our investigative problems in Norway differed to some extent from those in Sweden or Denmark. How can one study the reasons for the relative absence of suicide in a country? Is it not paradoxical to examine Norwegian suicidal patients for the purpose of finding out why there are not more suicides in Norway?

While it would have been of interest to conduct a thorough study of 25 Norwegian suicidal patients so as to have a comparable population to contrast with the Danish and Swedish groups, that reason alone might not have justified the work involved. Certainly I was interested in suicide in Norway and not merely in the reasons for its limitation. However, another determining factor was my hope of using the suicidal patients as an aid in constructing a picture of Norwegian psychosocial character and, through comparing it with psychosocial character in Denmark and Sweden, to work backward to the reasons for the low Norwegian suicide rate.*

Nevertheless, it was as much with the original questions in mind as for any other reason that the scope of the work was expanded in Norway. In addition to the thoroughly studied series of 25 suicidal patients, 15 non-suicidal patients and 12 non-patient nurses, relatives of almost all patients were interviewed, often several times. This procedure proved to be of

---

* It is possible, of course, that even if the picture of the Norwegian character is entirely correct, the deductions regarding the low Norwegian suicide rate may not be. Hence some of the typical Norwegian cases have been presented in more detail so that the reader has at least enough data to draw his own conclusions.

value as a further source of information. Another 20 patients were seen but not studied intensively. (All patients, relatives and non-patients were interviewed in Norwegian.)

In retrospect, it appears that it might have been possible to determine Norwegian psychosocial character and establish the reasons for the low suicide rate from the suicidal patients alone. However, it was reassuring to have other sources of information.*

In Denmark and Sweden observation was focused on the ways in which dependency was encouraged or discouraged, on the methods of discipline, the relations between the sexes, the attitudes toward work and success, the handling of aggression and general emotionality, and the individual attitudes toward death, dying and suicide. These factors were found to play a decisive role in shaping the character differences between Danes and Swedes and in determining the different reasons for the high suicide rates in the two countries. In order to obtain a comparable picture of the Norwegian character and to seek an explanation for the low suicide rate in Norway, it will be necessary to consider the same areas.

*   *   *

A 67 year old man took a combination of 60 to 70 tranquilizers and barbiturates. He was discovered in time by his neighbors who had become suspicious over the fact that he had not taken in his newspaper.

The patient became depressed when his second wife died of cancer six months previously. He constantly thought about her and frequently dreamt of her. He had "the hope, or perhaps more the wish" to see her again in an afterlife. In his dreams, which were always described as "pleasant," he and his wife

---

* It became clear after the work in Sweden that while psychological testing was helpful in individual cases, too many special problems were raised by the use of tests as a basis for cross-cultural comparisons with the Swedish results, at least within the framework of this project. Thus the psychologists who cooperated in Norway and Sweden have explored the possibilities of comparing their results. However, in this study psychological testing (Rorschach and TAT) was used only in ten of the Norwegian suicidal patients and only in situations where the tests were expected to be of some special value in a particular case.

would be on a trip together, at times accompanied by his mother.

He talked a great deal about his wife's kindness which had equaled that of his mother; how generously she cared for him and what a wonderful housekeeper she was. They had been married for 13 years following a nine year courtship. Their marriage had taken place a year after his mother's death, since he had not considered himself capable of caring for a wife, a son from his first marriage, and his mother.

The patient expressed the belief that he and his mother might have been overly attached to each other. He lost his father when he was eight years old. The patient's recollections of him were unpleasant: he was unfaithful, drank and mismanaged his financial affairs. The patient returned to his mother's home when he lost his first wife at the age of 27 and was left with a four year old son. He worked as a prison guard while his mother raised his son.

The patient's life with his mother was complicated by the fact that although generally kind, she was rather strong-willed and wanted to know when he had come home at night and what he had done while he was out. His story was at variance with that of his son who described him as a "house tyrant" and as inconsiderate of his mother. Since the patient resented any responsibility for his son, the latter was bitter toward his father and opposed his second marriage. Hence son and father had not been on speaking terms for a year prior to the stepmother's illness. On the whole the son's story was consistent with the patient's general description as aggressively domineering with women and yet at the same time as extremely dependent on them. For instance, although critical of the services rendered by his hospital nurse, he wanted to be praised by her because he ate well and did not smoke.

Before his suicide attempt the patient wrote a note to his son, in which he gave details of the possessions left to him. He also asked to be cremated and to have his ashes placed together with those of his mother. The only other time when he had seriously considered committing suicide was after his mother's death. When questioned regarding his request to be buried with his mother and not with his second wife, the patient stressed his desire not to hurt his son. The note was supposed to demonstrate that he had been both a good father and a good son.

Following his wife's death the patient lived alone in his neglected apartment. He emphasized several times that no woman could possibly replace his wife, but he seemed to have the unexpressed desire to find such a replacement. Although he had never been willing to have a housekeeper, he now decided to look for one. Three days after his suicide attempt he no longer appeared to be depressed. He liked to talk about his life and was inclined to be humorously ironical about himself. Apparently, with the air having been cleared by his suicide attempt, he was eager to begin living again.

Many of the Norwegian men who were determined to commit suicide reacted to some loss or threatened loss of a dependency object, thus resembling the Danish male patients. As a consequence, dreams and fantasies of reunion after death were almost as common in Norwegian as in Danish suicidal patients. This patient's awareness of his overdependence on his mother was typical of the attitudes of his group.

An extreme example of a man who remained overly attached to his mother was presented by a 62 year old, unmarried patient who still lived with his 81 year old mother. Although an engineer, he had not worked as such for many years because he was a heavy drinker. His alcoholism had been severe between the ages of 35 and 39, while he was involved in a serious affair with a young woman. His suicide attempt was directed at his mother who presumably had sent him—as he bitterly stated in his very first interview—to the hospital in order to get rid of him. She had had him locked up once before (an earlier admission related to his alcoholism) to interfere with his relationship with his girlfriend. His resentful complaints were that she held on to him, keeping him tied to her, but that she was sick and no longer able to take care of their apartment, to clean properly, etc. This patient liked to talk, too, although his primary objective was to justify his rather paranoid view of his life situation.

When his mother was interviewed, she made the impression of a strong personality possessed with dignity, grace and charm. She unwittingly confirmed her opposition to the girl that he had wanted to marry, but thought she had concealed her antagonism successfully. At any rate, she claimed that his drinking led to the breakup. She had cared for the patient all his life (he lost his father when he was seven years old) and described him as sweet and pleasant except when drunk or failing to get his own way. Even in his childhood any opposition provoked his anger, and she usually managed to handle him without openly opposing him. Having catered to him for over 60 years, she felt that her strength was giving out, so that she had finally wearied of her role.

Much of the patient's recent anxiety was in response to the aging and enfeeblement of his mother. To many Norwegian male patients with this type of problem it was not merely that the mother's death created an acute crisis, but that they tolerated poorly her terminal illness, often abandoning her at such a time.

Common in Norwegian patients with an overattachment to their mothers was such a combination of angry, tyrannical and dependent behavior. It differed from the more passive dependency that typified the Danish patients. The open dependent expression of an unbroken mother-son tie was significantly absent in Sweden.

The combination of alcoholism and suicidal tendency described above was observed in many Norwegian male suicidal patients. In 10 of the 14 male suicidal patients and in only two of the 11 females, alcohol was a definite problem. Apparently the psychodynamics of alcoholism and suicide overlap considerably in Norway. The following case is presented in some detail because the combination of alcoholism and suicidal preoccupation throws light on the particular Norwegian mother-son relationship.

A 61 year old man cut his wrists in the boarding house where he lived. He fell asleep and when he awoke in the hospital the next morning, he remembered the bloody sheets, but nothing else. An attempt 18 months earlier had been discovered almost immediately. In both instances, he had been drinking alone in his room, as had been his long-standing habit. In his first suicidal attempt he wished to give "a kick to life" and he "lay there and laughed" during the attempt. He did not know why he made this sudden and impulsive second attempt. Nevertheless, if he had a gun he would still wish to kill himself, but any other method would not be certain enough.

The patient admitted to being tired of living. He had no interest in his own thoughts or those of others. Life should be *harmonisk* (internally harmonious or tranquil—a state desired and admired by many patients and non-patients in Norway). Since his life had not been harmonious, there was no purpose in living. He believed in an afterlife where he would meet people with whom he would be in better harmony than with those whom he had known in life.

He related his life story and that of his suicide in a quiet way, neither appearing depressed nor seeking sympathy. He liked to talk about himself and was inclined to be detailed and circumstantial, occasionally laughing at his own foibles and at the same time trying to impress the interviewer with his intelligence.

During the past 37 years he had held a routine office job in a paper factory without much ambition. In his younger years he wanted to write "just to be able to express certain thoughts," but he had not succeeded with this plan. After work he would eat in a cafe before returning to his boarding house where he liked to listen to the radio, do some solitary drinking and go to bed. When he was younger, he had numerous friends and drank only in company. However, most of his friends had died during the war, so that he was now compelled to drink as a way of "escaping from time, which was boring."

Although he never married, he had had an active sexual life and even thought that he had been oversexed. He had lived with one woman for several years until he began to feel "like her property." Despite his interest in women, he became tired of them after sexual relations. When specifically questioned, he conceded that he missed being married, but only to the extent that he missed having coffee ready in the morning and food at night. His interests were intellectual and he never found a woman with whom he could talk.

He had grown up in a medium-sized town not far from Oslo. He spoke with some pride of his brother who was his senior by 18 months and had been successful in both his work and marriage. His sister was likewise married to a successful man and appeared to be happy with husband and children. The father had been a commercial artist with his own bookbinding firm and was praised by the patient for his talent, but disparaged in all other respects. He described his father as an alcoholic, who drank away his money and went into debt. He had other women and rarely ate with the family since he spent little time at home. He had died 21 years previously and the patient never felt like a son toward him.

His mother had been dead for only a year. When he discussed his own desire to die, the patient made no mention of her, although she was soon found to have been an integral part of his life situation. She had had a stroke eight months before her death and never fully recovered. Although the patient had visited her regularly all his life, he discontinued his visits after her stroke, because he could not bear witnessing her decline. Subsequently he did not want to visit her because he felt guilty over his negligent behavior.

Before his mother's illness he had always been close to her. When he was 12 or 13 years old, she discussed her marital difficulties with him, while the older son had run away from the home atmosphere. The mother had been an intelligent, well read woman, and the patient was inclined to compare other women unfavorably with her. He stressed that he had never been punished or reproached by his mother. When he moved to Oslo at the age of 19, he came home every weekend and spent every vacation there until he reached the age of 35. His relationship with his mother had been the only significant and meaningful one in his life. He recently became convinced that he had been too attached to her, but when she died he had no one, nor did he want to be attached to anyone else.

While in the hospital he had the following dream which he discussed on a subsequent visit as an outpatient: he was at a counter that looked like a bar. There was a jar on the counter, containing *sikkerhetsnåler* (literally—security pins; in English —safety pins). He had a strong desire to take one of the pins. At the side of the room there was a figure in black.

The patient saw at once the connection between his desire for a security pin, his desire for security and his addiction to alcohol. He spoke of his hospital pajamas as having been so big that he could have used a safety pin. This association led him back to the fact that he had wet his bed until he was 12 years old. Black, he said, suggested death to him and the black figure represented his mother. His attention in the dream had shifted back and forth from the desire for the pin to the woman.

Evidently he wanted to obtain from liquor what he expected from his mother in terms of security and solace, and he attempted to attain them either through drinking or death.

In addition to these last two patients there were two other single men over 30 in the suicide group. Both had lost their mothers within less than six months before their suicidal attempts and ascribed little or no significance to that loss, despite much evidence to the contrary.

The disruption in the mother-son relationship was by no means a potential threat only to the son. Several women in their sixties made suicide attempts following separation from their adult children. These mothers had not been happy with their husbands and had centered their lives around their children. The husband's death at an advanced age was apt to intensify their emotional demands on the children, and frustration of these demands could result in depression.

One of these women was 62 years old when she attempted to commit suicide while visiting her son in Oslo. The son had lived with his family in the same town as his parents, but a few years previously had moved to Oslo at his wife's insistence. From this time on, the patient's life had nothing to offer, except to take care of her ailing and senile husband and to run his business. When she visited her son the first time in Oslo, it was the prospect of having to go back home to her husband that motivated her suicide attempt. Her husband had been very good to her and in earlier years had been "like a father." However, upon the birth of her son, her whole interest was focused on him, although she was unable to explain why she so eagerly abandoned the role of a wife for that of a mother. Apparently she now had the same interest in her son's children. The ambivalent mixture of her feelings was revealed in a recent dream, in which she was driving a car. Her grandson was with her and fell out of the car. According to her story she always was as worried about injury to her grandchildren as she had been about accidents while raising her son. In such circumstances the women tended to repress anger toward their children, while that toward their husbands was openly expressed in the form of hostility and conscious death wishes.

The close ties between mother and son and the importance of dependency loss in precipitating whatever suicide does occur in Norway, made the Norwegian suicidal patients appear somewhat similar to those in Denmark. However, this comparison is only partly true.

Five of the 14 males lost a parent during the first eight years of their lives. Two others were born illegitimately and had no contact with their fathers. Three had fathers described as alcoholic, unfaithful and shiftless. Three had clearly been unwanted by at least one parent, and there was only one case in which no such trauma was uncovered. The Norwegian suicidal patients had more traumatic life histories than was true for the other Norwegian patients or non-patients. So marked a disparity in the severity of emotional trauma between the histories of suicidal and non-suicidal people was not observed in Sweden or Denmark, which may be only another way of saying that more adversity was necessary to precipitate a suicide in Norway than in the other two countries.

The loss or absence of a parent early in life was shown by Zilboorg[1] to be correlated with a tendency to suicide. In our cases, the absent father also further induced the mother to center her emotional interest on her son.

Irrespective of these traumatic events, the histories of suicidal patients accurately reflected a tendency on the part of Norwegian women to build their emotional lives around their children. This tendency will later be shown to exist in the other female patients and nurses regardless of whether or not there was an absent father or unhappy marriage. It may be noted that in comparable situations Swedish women could not console themselves with their children.

As a rule, Norwegian and Danish mothers differ significantly in expressing the mother-child tie. The Norwegian child is given much physical freedom to play and run around, while the Danish child is not. Fresh air is almost worshipped in Norway, and young children are out playing for long hours, unsupervised or watched only by older siblings. Norwegian mothers are more like Swedish mothers in that they want to have a self-sufficient and independent child. Contrary to Danish mothers, they will stress how early their child can walk or talk or be alone. While the mother may center her emotional life on the child, she will generally allow the child to have physical freedom. She will try to derive happiness from the child's independent accomplishments and live vicariously through them. This contradiction between tying the child to her and yet wishing to have an independent child dominates Norwegian mother-child relations. On the one hand, there is the tendency to infantilize the child or, as one child psychiatrist described it, "to put a chocolate in the child's mouth rather than to answer his question." On the other hand, the mother tends to make a relatively young child her confidant. By revealing her marital dissatisfactions to the child, she is likely to overtax his emotional strength.

The net result of these mixed attitudes is a less dependent, less passive child (or adult) than is found in Denmark. Together with the Norwegian child's greater freedom of aggression to be discussed later, his greater independence leads to a marked difference between the Norwegian and Danish character structures. It may also make for a lesser suicidal vulnerability to dependency loss in the Norwegian than in the Dane.

                    ❋   ❋   ❋

What both suicidal and non-suicidal patients as well as the nurses revealed about the relations between men and women in Norway was of interest in itself and also because it threw light on the nature of the Norwegian mother-child relationship.

A 34 year old successful engineer took 25 sleeping pills the day after separating from his wife and three children. He had taken an interest in a girl, much younger than himself, who worked in the same office. He informed his wife by telephone of his suicide plan and in this manner was "saved" in plenty of time.

Several weeks prior to this suicide attempt the patient had his first sexual relations with his girlfriend, who apparently was a virgin. While she wished to marry him, he wanted to wait a while. Hence when he left his wife, he went to live with his father.

The patient and his wife were the same age. They had been married for seven years and had known each other five years longer. According to his report he had not really been in love with her when they married, but felt obliged to marry her since they had been going steady during the best years of their lives. Although he first denied any intention to place the blame on his wife, he stated later that she was "all for the children" and that he had always been secondary. Presumably their relationship had been better before a son was born after their first year of marriage. Things became worse after the birth of twin daughters three years later. In his opinion, his wife was too domineering and usually made decisions without consulting him, despite his protests. When asked whether or not his girlfriend was domineering, he replied, "She is not for the time being, but you never know how she will turn out." Subsequently it became clear, however, that his girlfriend was less inclined than his wife to take initiative and that he, as a consequence, took more initiative with her.

At home he had begun to drink quite heavily two or three times a week. He was reluctant at first to connect the drinking with his marriage, although it had been going on for four years, that is, as long as his marriage was in difficulty. During the subsequent months, while he remained separated from his wife, he did no drinking.

As to his suicide attempt, he eventually admitted that he probably did not wish to die but wanted to ease his conscience. By painfully showing his wife that he did not take their separation lightly, he hoped to justify his plan to remain separated from her and to develop the relationship with his girlfriend.

The patient was fearful of women and expected to be disappointed by them, since he lost his mother at the age of three. His father was very strict and had little to do with the children. He hired a woman to raise them, and his only contact with the children served the purpose of pressing them to do well in school. Since he was a teacher, the patient expected to receive help and guidance from him, but he remained frustrated in this hope. An older brother, who was outstanding in school, was the father's favorite, although the patient was likewise successful in school and in his job. His work was not even affected by his recent emotional crisis.

When interviewed, the patient's wife was found to be intelligent and cooperative, with a fairly good capacity for introspection. She defended herself against the complaint of being too domineering by pointing to the fact that he took no initiative in their social planning, leaving everything to her. Of even greater interest was her confirmation of his statement that their relationship changed after the birth of the first child, and her willingness to accept the responsibility for this change. Upon her return from the hospital she felt estranged and had no sexual desire for him. She had the feeling that there was a circle drawn around the boy and herself and that her husband was somehow outside it. However, even prior to this event she had experienced sexual pleasure only to a limited extent.

Having been 27 years old at the time of her marriage, she wanted a child right away, while he wished to wait a little longer. She worked until three weeks before delivery and then missed her work. She claimed to have been in love with her husband when she married him, but later they had drifted apart. She admitted that she may have initiated the dissension, but considered that his "childish jealousy" of the child aggravated the situation. She resented his lack of interest in the boy and bitterly complained at one point in the interview that he never got up to care for the children. Her rest was not considered; only his was important.

Complaints that their wives subordinated everything to the children and were domineering and critical were frequently voiced by Norwegian men. One further example of such complaints may be presented here.

A 53 year old man attempted suicide about 18 months after separation from his wife, to whom he had been married for 25 years. She had been openly unfaithful to him many times before and during their marriage. Actually, he married her because she was pregnant and he believed, although not without some doubt, that he was the father of the child. Throughout their marriage she was critical of him. He was an increasingly severe alcoholic and she finally insisted upon separation.

During the night before his suicide attempt the patient had the following dream: he was on a railroad trip with his wife. The train was crowded and there was little standing room. They were talking together and the conversation was pleasant.

His association with regard to the train was that death is often pictured as a journey or trip. His association to the crowd on the train was that they had been young people, and it induced him to talk about his children. He had always felt that he was in the way at home. The children did not listen to him, since his wife had encouraged them to ignore him. Nevertheless, he would have liked to be reunited with his family, although he had given up all hope. Even in his dream of reunion in death, the children interfered.

Few Norwegian women were as candid as the wife of the patient who reported that a circle excluding her husband was drawn around herself and her child from the time of his birth. Nevertheless, her reaction was probably a common one.

The Norwegian nurses confirmed the view of the woman's role as that of a mother rather than a wife.* Questioned about the qualities that an ideal woman should have, they invariably spoke of domestic abilities and affection for children, never mentioning any qualities that a woman should have in relation to a man. Even when this omission was pointed out to them, Norwegian nurses had difficulty with this question, while Swedish and American nurses emphasized the relationship with the man.

One particular objective of Norwegian suicidal women was to resolve their unsatisfied dependency longings in their relationship with the children. Failure in this respect tended to be crucial in precipitating their suicide attempts. A few case histories may illustrate the extent to which the child becomes the focus of the woman's interests and difficulties. At the same time they will show that disappointment in men also enters the picture, frequently followed by ambivalence toward the child.

A 27 year old married nurse took 30 sleeping pills while her husband was out drinking. She expected that he would be too intoxicated upon return to notice how deeply she slept. He was drunk when he came home, but noticed her condition nevertheless and asked someone to take her to the hospital. She had intended to die, but now was uncertain about it. She believed in God and hoped for an afterlife.

The patient's marriage was her second and had lasted five years. She regarded her husband's drinking as the main source of their difficulties. They had been separated for most of the year, but two weeks before the suicide attempt she had taken him back with the stipulation that he stop drinking. However, he continued to drink and refused to move out, although she hoped that he would now do so. He blamed his drinking on

---

* Nic Waal [2] makes a similar point about the Norwegian woman in her role as wife and mother.

her refusal to bear him a child, while she did not want to have a child with him because of his drinking. He used to drink before his marriage, but it became worse afterwards.

When questioned about her own role in the marital difficulties, she admitted having been somewhat cold and unaffectionate. She would submit sexually to him, but without pleasure. She could neither discuss her personal problems with him nor offer him much comfort regarding his own. Although she had loved him, she had gone into this second marriage with considerable doubt. She now wanted to get rid of her husband and was determined to have nothing to do with men any more. Her entire life had been disrupted by her father who, when she was only 11 years old, had left her mother for another woman. Subsequently the patient was sent from place to place and did not live again with either parent although both remarried. As an adult she distrusted all men and never believed them when they professed to love her.

From her first marriage she had an eight year old boy, whom she took to her mother's house in the country before she attempted to commit suicide. While under the effect of the pills, she had the following dream: she was dead and the boy was at her mother's. She was telling him that she would not come back to him. She tearfully stated that he seemed so distant. In connection with this dream she confirmed her feeling that she was far away from her son—he lived in his own world. He fluctuated between being nice and being stubborn, and at times he had attacks of rage—particularly directed at her. He had difficulties in adjusting to school, although he was bright.

Her first marriage at the age of 18 was with a man five years older and became necessary when she expected this child. Her son looked like her first husband, but was kinder than his father, who proved to be quite cruel. In her opinion she married him out of spite—to get away from her home situation and to show her family that she could be happy. She thought that she had been fond of her child, although at first she did not want him. Her second husband liked her son and was good to him when he was sober. When inebriated he so frightened the boy that the patient would not take her son back from her mother until he moved out. She even thought that the boy might be better off with her mother, who had more time for him and was devoted to him. The patient herself worked at night as a nurse's aide, slept during the day and was always tired.

In our last talk in the hospital the patient reported that her husband had visited her the day before and had agreed to move out. That night she had the following dream: she had a sick baby to care for. The baby belonged to her sister-in-law, who had abandoned the child. The dream was unpleasant, because there was much to do for the child, with whom something seemed to be wrong. In this dream she was free of her husband, but struggled with the thought that she wanted to be free of her child as well.

When partly because of dissatisfaction with the husband, the child—and it is usually the male child—becomes the woman's emotional focus, some of the anger toward the husband is likely to spill over into the relationship with the child, giving it an ambivalent quality. Inability to tolerate such aggressive feelings toward the child often leads to a reactive overinvolvement with him. Difficulties in handling and controlling a child's aggression frequently follow, so that the extremely dependent, tyrannical child is one of the most common problems in Norwegian child psychiatry clinics.

Suicidal complications tend to occur in those women whose own dependency frustrations are so pronounced that their resentment at caring for their children exceeds their capacity for handling it. The following case illustrates the effect of a woman's anger and frustration with her husband upon her feelings toward her child.

The patient was 34 years old when she made her suicide attempt a few weeks after separation from her second husband. She had been married for four years to a man who was three years younger. In addition to two children from her first marriage, she had two children—a four year old boy and a three year old girl—in her second marriage. Her husband was good, except for the fact that he disliked the two older children. He criticized them on every occasion and wanted them out of the house, especially when he had to support them after their father's death two years previously. The patient left him because of his dislike for these two children.

She was only 19 when she married her first husband, who proved to be an epileptic and was also unfaithful. She had

felt misunderstood by both husbands. She disliked sexual relations with either of them and had never enjoyed sex—she merely
tolerated it. She related tearfully that in both marriages the man
had insisted on having sexual relations with her on the first day
after her return from the maternity ward.

Shortly before her suicide attempt she dreamt that her four
year old son was drowned. This boy had been the most difficult
of her children. He refused to go out and continually clung
to her. She described him as resembling her husband in that
he became angry easily and had to have his way. Her anger
toward both her husband and their son was clearly inter-
connected.

Her husband wanted her back, but she had no desire to return. On the contrary, this patient's suicide attempt amounted
to an act of riddance in that the dramatization of her own suffering provided her with a justification for leaving him. In general Norwegian women did not use their suicidal act as frequently as their Swedish or Danish counterparts for coercive
purposes, especially that of forcing a man to return. The employ-
ment of suicide as a kind of emotional blackmail to arouse guilt
or to force affection was encountered in the majority of female
suicide attempts in Denmark and Sweden, while such cases
were in the minority in Norway.

In line with this difference, Norwegian patients did not present
their stories with a view to arousing sympathy or pity as many
Danish patients did. Only some of the nurses and patients had
histories like the Danish patients; namely, that they had primarily been disciplined through the mother's tears or by being
made to feel that she had been hurt by their misbehavior.
More frequently they were scolded and sometimes spanked
or they were not allowed to go out.

The histories of the two female patients—a 17 year old girl
and a 32 year old divorced woman—each of whom made a suicide
attempt to force a man to return to her, may be briefly mentioned
here. In the case of the young girl, her parents were divorced
when she was nine years old, and she had seen her father only
twice since that time. She was engaged to marry a 30 year old
man, but her fiancé had recently been in favor of breaking their
engagement. Her suicide attempt was made with 50 diabinase

tablets and nearly killed her through hypoglycemia, but it did bring her fiancé back.

Once her boyfriend had returned, she derived little emotional or sexual pleasure from their relationship. She spoke and dreamt of having children right away, in the hope that caring for them would make her happy and somehow revitalize her feelings for the boyfriend. Her dreams of having children had a sad, disappointing quality and were probably an accurate anticipation of her future reaction. Nevertheless, she managed to become pregnant in order to accelerate forcibly their marriage plans.

When she discussed her suicide attempt in more detail, it became clear that the desire to bring her fiancé back was only part of her motivation. Equally important was her protest that if it had to come to a rejection or desertion, she would be the one to do it. Death by suicide would accomplish this goal for her, and her suicide attempt was very much in the nature of a retaliatory abandonment.*

The 32 year old woman worked in an institution for retarded children where she had an affair with one of her co-workers. When he abandoned her for another woman, she attempted to commit suicide in order to punish him, to reproach him and hopefully to bring him back. The last objective was not accomplished, since her boyfriend was not influenced by her attempt. She also came from a broken home. Her parents were divorced when she was nine years old, and whatever recollections of a home life she had were unpleasant because of her parents' frequent quarrels and her father's heavy drinking. She went on to develop a way of life which was characterized by unhappy love relationships. Her last affair was only one in a long series of such failures. She had once been married for a short time and had a child that was raised by her in-laws after her divorce. She was so sensitive about having given away her child that she broke off the interviews when she was pressed for a complete account of her feelings in this matter.

It may be noted that even in these two suicidal patients, conflicting attitudes toward children played an important role in

---

* Retaliatory abandonment as a motivation for suicide is discussed in more detail in the earlier chapter dealing with the psychodynamics of suicide.

their psychological picture. Moreover, in both cases the over-reaction to the loss of a man was influenced by the special vulnerability to abandonment found in girls who have lost their fathers early in life.

In view of the fact that a Norwegian woman handles her dependency needs in relation to her children and thereby reduces her expectations of the man, she is likely to be less vulnerable to disappointment in a man or loss of the man. Thus, while she may in some ways resemble her Danish cousin, she is actually less vulnerable to the depressive effects of a disappointing love relationship. This fact is of some consequence with respect to the frequency of suicide. While the male suicide rate in Denmark averages nearly three times the corresponding Norwegian one, the suicide rate for Danish women is about five times as high as that for Norwegian women.

In Norway women's magazine stories* give a picture of the female that is very much in keeping with the one that has been described here. As is true for the woman in Danish stories, her maternal virtues and her devotion to her children are strongly accented. However, the heroine in Danish magazine stories is depicted as helpless and yearning to be cared for by someone, and this is not true of the Norwegian heroine. Nor is the Norwegian heroine, like her Swedish counterpart, preoccupied with the constant fear of losing her man. The Norwegian stories are focused on such problems as health, money and alcohol, while love between men and women receives less emphasis and is treated more matter-of-factly than in Swedish and Danish stories.

✿   ✿   ✿

Usually the married female patients who have been described tolerated sexual relations with little pleasure and some feeling

---

* Most Norwegian stories are actually taken from Danish and Swedish magazines and only the names and places are changed. Only stories by Norwegian authors have been used to analyze recurrent Norwegian themes. Despite the exchange of stories among the three countries, it has not been difficult to pick out the thematic material that characterizes stories by authors from each of the three countries. After the first 50 or so stories, my co-reader and I were able to say on the basis of the theme whether a given story was by a Swede, Norwegian or Dane. A later check on the author's nationality showed us to have been right in over 90 per cent of the cases.

of being exploited. Complaints that the man was interested only in sex and failed to be reassuring, tender or loving enough, were typical. The men generally accepted their wives' sexual unresponsiveness with resignation. One male patient had a moderately severe potency problem, several others had some potency anxiety of varying degrees, and many functioned sexually without conscious anxiety but with limited pleasure. However, since Norwegian women were inclined to complain about excessive sexual demands, they were rather indifferent to the man's sexual inadequacy or neglect.

The sexual histories of the Norwegian nurses varied considerably and were similar to those of American Protestant nurses. With the exception of one nurse whose father was a doctor, all of them complained that they had received no sexual education from their parents, and in this respect were like the Norwegian patients. The child's sexual activity is prohibited and its existence is denied in the same manner as was observed in Sweden and Denmark. Masturbation is discouraged by such remarks as "a nice child sleeps with his hands on top of the covers." Parental disapproval of sexual activity is conveyed to the child through avoidance of the subject or through derogatory statements about "other girls" who are "too free" sexually. As a rule Norwegian parents let their adolescent children find their own way, and there were many references to the inability of teenagers to obtain any parental advice on sexual and other personal matters. The extent of sexual activity among the unmarried seemed about the same as was inferred for the rest of Scandinavia. In Norway, too, young couples who are engaged or going steady are somewhat less inclined to conceal sexual activity than is customary in the United States.

On the whole, early dependency frustrations, the reaction to the favored position generally reserved for male children and the inadequacies of the father's role in the home play as significant a part as sexual education and experience in shaping the girl's attitude toward her own sexual role. Some of the material presented by nurses may illustrate this point.

One young nurse talked about her father, who was a teacher, and habitually discussed political and philosophical questions in a rambling manner. She first claimed that she had admired him because he always seemed so certain of his views. She later added, however, that she had learnt from her mother to pretend interest in what he said: "We actually laughed at papa. My brother and I would kick each other under the table." The "pretending" extended to other areas as well. Although definitely on the stingy side, her father liked to believe, and wanted his family to believe, that he was generous. He insisted on having everything in the house in its proper place, and he was equally determined that things always be done at a certain time. Meals had to be precisely on schedule, as did his nap after the main meal. "It was impossible for him to say or think something upon impulse. If on occasion he was angry, he breathed heavily like an animal."

The daughter believed that in many ways she was like her father rather than her more lively mother. She was, in fact, rambling in her speech and seldom spontaneous. Although she presumably wanted to have a man whom she could respect, she had rebelled against any expression of firmness, initiative or anger or against any signs of assertive masculinity on the part of her former fiancé.

Her father's circumstantiality was characteristic of some of the previously described patients. His insistence on adherence to routine was not unusual and reflected a petty demonstration of power in an otherwise ineffectual man rather than true obsessiveness. At the time of middle age, however, such a pattern may be so entrenched that some of these men tend to live only by order and routine with a minimum of pleasure. In his refusal to be disturbed during his nap, this girl's father did not go as far as those men listed in the Oslo telephone directory with the notice "Do not call from 3 to 5 P.M.," intended to protect their afternoon nap.

Living by ritual cannot be more clearly described than it is in the account of Bureau Chief Ribe in Sigurd Hoel's *A Day in October.*[3] "Bureau Chief Ribe came home for dinner at half past three as usual," is the way in which he is introduced to the reader. "Punctually at a quarter to four the Bureau Chief sat down to dinner." He becomes irritated because his wife has not put the salt shaker in its proper place. "At half past four the Bureau Chief left the table. No need to look at the clock, it was half past four." . . . "He always undressed and had an hour's nap after dinner. There was no need for anyone to wake him. He always awoke at the stroke of half past five, dressed and made his way to the lavatory—not because he thought it was any use, but on principle. The Bureau Chief suffered from constipation."

Seven of the 12 nurses classified their mothers as the stronger parent who had made the decisions, and the same was true for the majority of male and female patients. Feelings varying from a lack of idealization of the father to open disrespect or contempt were common, and many of the nurses reported that they had taken over this attitude from their mothers.

The Norwegian nurses' and patients' description of the ineffective father as a person to be humored and who can easily be outwitted is reflected in the Norwegian folk tales recorded by Asbjørnsen and Moe.[4] The king of the tales is usually fat, ineffective and far from being a figure of authority. While the trolls are more intimidating, their defeat is a certainty. With the help of the princess of the tale, Askeladden outwits and destroys them with relative ease.

Some of the nurses remarked that they wanted a man who would tell them what to do.* It was quite clear, however, they were not involved with such men and really did not wish to be. A few other nurses stated frankly that a woman was expected to appear submissive, even if she happened to be stronger than the man.

One nurse who was soon to be married reported the following dream in our last session: she came to a place that was poorly furnished and housed a little boy who was completely wet. She had to lie in bed next to him in order to take care of him.

Her plan was to give up nursing after her marriage and to help her husband on his farm where she would also be responsible for the care of his ailing parents. She did not openly complain about her future life, but her associations anticipated a rather hard and bleak existence, and the place in the dream was clearly her fiancé's farm. The little boy was her fiancé

---

* It is this kind of remark that Rodnick[5] quotes and accepts as indicating that Norwegian women are extremely submissive and characteristically dominated by their men. Eliot and Hillman,[6] in their sociological study of Norway, avoid this pitfall by picturing the woman's role economically, socially and in terms of status while recognizing that "more detailed and intimate studies of family interaction" are needed to define the woman's role within the family.

who actually was 35 years old, while she herself was 28. The defensive maneuver of handling the relationship with a man, and the sexual relationship in particular, by picturing the man as a child and thus not a threat, was observed in many Norwegian nurses and female patients.

This particular nurse grew up on a farm with four other children. Since her father was a whale fisherman and frequently away from home, her mother had to do the farmwork. As the oldest girl, she had to take care of the three younger children. The oldest son was the mother's favorite and was excused from this task. She claimed to be fond of children and to have always desired to become a children's nurse. However, she recalled a recurrent nightmare in her childhood and thereby revealed how angry she had been at her younger siblings and her mother, because her own dependency needs had been frustrated. In the dream she had to care for an unpleasant young child who ran away from her and fell over a cliff. In different versions of this dream the child was injured, killed, or saved by being transformed into a bird and flying away.

In her early teens she helped in a store and became attached to the owner's sick wife, while acting as her nurse. One of the major themes of her dreams dealt with a plan to discontinue her work at the hospital and to go back to this couple's place. She would again work in the store and care for the woman, and this prospect was always pleasant.

Another recurrent theme in this girl's dreams helped in the understanding of her emotional life. In her teens she had nightmares in which she was pursued by men and had to run for her life. As she grew older, she was chased by animals and no longer by men. More recently she usually managed to save herself from the animals by changing into a bird and flying away. When not seen as helpless children, men frightened her. Transformation of the men into animals and of herself into a bird symbolized her running away from them. She was characterized by a certain degree of emotional aloofness and appeared to be prepared for her future life. It was doubtful that any future disappointment would be a surprise to her.

Such fears of men were typical of the nurses. As was seen in this girl, early dependency frustrations played a crucial part in determining their fears of the female role. Of equal importance were their hostilities toward the father and adoption of the mother's disrespect for him. When both were combined, sexual fears were particularly pronounced. Attempts to infantilize the man were the most common form of defense against such fears. Infantilization was also used as a defense by American nurses, but not nearly as often as by the Norwegian ones. In general, identification with the masculine role and open competition with men were more prevalent in the American than in the Norwegian nurses.

✻   ✻   ✻

Characteristically, Norwegians have their own ways of dealing with aggression. First of all they have more freedom in verbalizing and expressing it than is true for Danes and Swedes. Such remarks as "I don't wish to blame others" or "I feel guilty about speaking badly about my wife" or "It's not right to speak about someone who isn't here to defend himself" were often made. However, they merely served as an introduction to open expressions of hostility and were not indicative of real feelings of guilt or any particular inhibitions.

Openly angry patients were more common in Norway than in the other two countries. If they did not like a question or the way in which an interview was conducted, Norwegian patients were likely to become angry and refuse to talk. Such reactions as just walking out of the room occurred half a dozen times in Norwegian patients and never in the interviews of Danish or Swedish patients. In Norway patients made little effort in the tone of their voice or in their words, movements and facial expressions to disguise their anger.

The Norwegian way of handling aggression is typified by the word *forurettet* which implies anger over unfair treatment. The word exists in Swedish, too, but is used only infrequently there. In Norway it is one of the commonest and most essential terms in the description of psychiatric problems. Angry feelings can be nursed, are readily justified, and can be used for retaliatory purposes.

One 42 year old married man was admitted to the hospital with symptoms of severe anxiety and feelings of depersonalization. He felt strongly *forurettet* toward his mother-in-law.

He had been married for seven years to a woman who was seven years his senior. He had known her for nine years before their marriage, but he did not marry her until he had completed his legal studies. Following their marriage they moved into a one-room house on his mother-in-law's property. He complained bitterly that his mother-in-law was domineering and that his wife listened to her.

For a period of four years his wife and son had lived in the larger house with his mother-in-law, who was ailing and needed help and care. The patient went there only to eat and then returned to his own place to sleep. Although the mother-in-law had recently been very sick, the patient was extremely bitter over the fact that his wife had neglected him and had concentrated attention on her mother.

When he was asked again and again why he had shown so little resistance to his wife's moving out, a different picture emerged. He had not been able to cope with his wife's moodiness. Discouraged by varying degrees of sexual impotence, he doubted that he ever really loved her and therefore preferred to live alone.

Of course, he was hiding much of his angry reaction to his wife behind his complaints about his abusive mother-in-law and her domination of her daughter. For seven years he had handled this situation by establishing some sort of neurotic equilibrium. His mother-in-law's illness and imminent death had threatened this equilibrium, but not in the originally suggested manner (with his wife spending too much time with her mother). Actually he was faced with the loss of his mother-in-law who served as the focus of his paranoid system of adaptation. While she was ill, it had been difficult for him to be justifiably angry, and her death was certain to deprive him of the main outlet for his anger. In fact, he would then be compelled to deal actively with the real problems in his marriage.

A 61 year old woman blamed her suicide attempt on her husband's infidelity and stated that she no longer had anything to live for. Her husband had recently been in the habit of coming home late without a reason, although he always denied an interest in other women. She rambled about various incidents without furnishing any conclusive evidence. Although he had previously been faithful to her, they had no sexual relations during the past year, presumably because of "falling genital organs" which caused her pain. She had never enjoyed sexual relations with him, but had previously acquiesced. In her third interview she expressed the hope that he would find companionship with a stable middle-aged woman who could no longer bear a child. She was afraid that a younger girl would be too wild and might become pregnant, thus forcing him to abandon his family. Most of her talk, and she hardly paused for breath, revolved around the unfairness and injustice of his recent attitude toward her. She had been a good wife—always saved money and had plenty of food ready for him.

Although she originally portrayed herself as the long-suffering wife, the picture soon changed. Apparently she had badgered her husband to obtain a confession of his infidelity, following which he would be permitted to do as he pleased. Then she would be entitled to the house which she wanted to have for herself and eventually for her married daughter. For four or five months they had talked about divorce, but he wanted her to move out. Evidently she had to be the "injured party," although she had never been in love with him. She complained that he was neither affectionate nor tender and that he was only interested in her sexually.

She accused him of provoking an argument with her when he wished to go out for an evening. When she had become angry, he would say that he could not stand it any longer and had to go out. Thus she was accusing him (apparently without any justification according to her own family) of using the same device that she had employed.

The patient had never mingled with people other than her family. Her husband, at her insistence, had to make his social visits and take his vacations alone throughout their marriage. Matrimony had always been a strain on her, and her real desire was to be alone. All she wanted was to eat, to sleep and to work in the garden around her house. However, she had to feel sufficiently abused in order to justify this final renunciation of her husband. Her suicide attempt served this function, as it did for other suicidal patients in Norway. As a victim and a sufferer, she felt entitled to take action against her tormentor and to free herself of him.

The male counterpart of this case was a 31 year old, married garbage collector who attempted to hang himself. He was unconscious and cyanotic and apparently only one minute or two away from death, when his wife who had visited a neighbor returned earlier than expected and cut him down. As a child he had been given by his mother to another woman, who raised him together with her own children, without cruelty, but strictly and with little affection. He held a strong animosity toward women, but had little justification for the anger directed at his wife, since she was affectionate, kind and indulgent. After eight years of marriage he began to accuse her of infidelity or at least of sexual desire for her brother-in-law. Many of the patient's own dreams dealt with affairs with other women and were patently covered up by his accusations. He tried hard to convince himself of his wife's imaginary affair, but had to give up after a year.

Unable to feel properly justified in his anger, he became depressed and increasingly preoccupied with the fear of lung cancer. He regarded cancer as a destructive, consuming disease, and he was figuratively choked by his consuming and destructive feelings toward his wife. She revealed that twice before his attempt to hang himself he had "playfully" pretended to choke her.

Although these three patients were unsuccessful in managing their aggression through feeling *forurettet*, their histories serve to illustrate the function of this adaptive maneuver and some of the uses to which it was put by Norwegian patients. For the majority of both patients and non-patients, feeling *forurettet* was of assistance to them in managing their aggression.

The tendency to feel abused and justifiably angry and to hold on to this anger expressed itself in different ways. Slights are not easily forgiven, nor is it uncommon that former friends cease talking to each other and become life-long enemies. Norwegian farmers are notoriously litigious and forever involved in wrangles over property boundaries or hunting and fishing rights. They are often amateur lawyers and even those who have not been in court themselves can cite cases and precedents.

The Norwegian method of handling their understandable anger at the Germans was also characteristic. It was noticeable everywhere, and on a bus or in a restaurant one could hear Norwegians complain about "unwelcome German tourists." When in discussing Germany with colleagues, reference was made to German cultural accomplishments, the immediate response was that most of the positive contributions that Germany had made to the world had come from German Jews, and this argument was supplemented by a long list ranging from Einstein to Freud.

The Norwegian patients and non-patients made many references to World War II. A young nurse recalled the terror caused by the presence of an armed German soldier demanding food at her parents' farm. Although no one was hurt, the memory of her frightened parents remained in the girl's mind, and all her nightmares dealt with German soldiers. Memories of this kind were common among nurses and patients over the age of 25, and the war was spontaneously mentioned in many of their stories: a patient who had been arrested during a student demonstration at the university, another who might have forgiven his former wife's infidelity, but not with a German soldier, etc.

While wartime experiences were brought up by the patients and nurses, at social gatherings there were frequent expressions of resentment toward the Germans or humor at their expense. In contrast to the Danes, for whom the Germans were a subject that they wished to forget, the Norwegians enjoyed the opportunity of referring to and disparaging the Germans. Nor could this difference be explained simply by the fact that Norway had been more seriously affected by the war than Denmark.[7] Although the Norwegian attitude was understandable, the tendency to keep alive their animosity and even derive some pleasure from it was consistent with the national pattern of nursing anger. There is also the Norwegian animosity toward Swedes, which has its roots in Sweden's hegemony in Norway prior to 1905. With the people's envy of Swedish wealth and their resentment at Sweden's role in World War II, that animosity is also expressed frequently and with some satisfaction. Here, however, it is tempered by admiration for Swedish accomplishments.

The nursing of justifiable anger is less important psychodynamically than the ability to feel *forurettet* as a convenient excuse for pre-existing anger. It is at least psychologically consistent that while Danish psychopathology tends to be on the depressive and Swedish on the schizoid side, Norwegian pathology is characterized by paranoid features.

Norwegian children are permitted to express aggression toward other youngsters in striking contrast to the rules for Danish and Swedish children. It is considered legitimate and desirable for boys to fight back physically until they reach an age of 11 to 12. In particular, parents encourage their boys to fight back in situations where the child seems to have been unfairly treated by another child. Thus the child learns early that if he is the aggrieved party he can count on parental support, and he soon learns how to present himself as the aggrieved party. Girls are not supposed to fight physically, but otherwise they develop essentially the same patterns of dealing with their anger.

From the age of 12 the situation changes. The Norwegian adult can still be angry, but an uncontrolled or noisy expression of anger in the Latin manner will make the offender seem crude and ridiculous. Political cartoons in Norway will satirize someone merely through depicting and exaggerating his uncontrolled anger and consequent crudeness.

Norwegian cartoons* are instructive not only in content, but also by revealing the manner in which aggression is expressed. A child is reproached by an adult because his bicycle is blocking the sidewalk or because he has been impolite in some other way. The child responds with some variation of "Kiss my behind!" and this response is a prototype of hundreds of Norwegian cartoons. The child's aggression may often be unprovoked, and the humor will simply lie in its unabashed expression toward adults in situations where they are normally respected or obeyed. The adult reader has apparently no difficulty in identifying with this form of aggression, which is disguised only by the fact that it is expressed by a child. Children are used in cartoons to make open

---

* These comments are based on the study of over a thousand Norwegian cartoons by Hammarlund, Hetland, Blix, Pedro, Imsland and Nilssen. Norwegian humorists such as Stabel and Aukrust, whose cartoons are only a part of their text, have not been included in this discussion, since their work cannot be readily compared with the more widely used straight cartoon form.

attacks on such adult institutions as the educational system, the government or the clergy. If the attack is made by adults, a *forurettet* quality is injected into the cartoon. However, if someone of low social status attacks someone of a much higher status, the status difference alone may be sufficient provocation to justify the aggression.

More bitterness is expressed in the relationship between the sexes. While the woman is often drawn with a wide open mouth and in the act of making excessive economic demands in an angry or quarrelsome manner, the man is shown as passive and resigned. The male reader is thus readily enabled to feel justified in his own aggression in a comparable situation.

Apart from revealing the various methods of expressing aggression, Norwegian cartoons reflect a relative freedom in the expression of aggression, thus confirming the picture presented by Norwegian patients and nurses (nine of the 12 nurses reported that in childhood they could freely express aggression toward parents, siblings and other children, and it was clear that they carried this freedom into adulthood). The ability of Norwegians to feel justifiably angry and to express their aggression openly made it less necessary for them to internalize anger. It is to be recalled that retroflexion of anger was a characteristic feature of Danish and Swedish patients and was found to play an important role in the causation of suicide in both of these countries.

*   *   *

The relative freedom enjoyed by Norwegian patients in the expression of anger created the impression that they were generally less restrained in expressing emotions than were the Swedish or Danish patients. However, despite the fact that many Norwegians were free to reveal their inner feelings, there were signs that they had difficulty in showing emotions. Blushing was as common in Norwegian nurses as it was in the Swedish nurses. The ironic humor with which Norwegian male patients presented their emotional problems appeared to be a socially acceptable way of revealing inner feelings without excessive anxiety or loss of emotional control.

While about 50 per cent of the Norwegian patients liked to verbalize their feelings and were easily induced to talk about themselves, some of their talking had an obsessional quality and was intended as much to conceal as to reveal. Very few were as emotionally detached as was common in Sweden.

A few suicidal patients were similar to those in Sweden in that they regarded themselves as emotionally dead. However, the Norwegian symptom of deadness usually occurred as a manifestation of a severe depression precipitated by abandonment, and not as that life-long feeling of affective deadness shown by many Swedish patients. The Norwegian type of deadness was most clearly presented by two men, who had histories of severe emotional deprivation in childhood and became alcoholics. Both had been married for many years and made their suicide attempts after they had been deserted by their wives. One patient viewed death as a possible relief from his feeling of deadness. He dreamt of doctors dissecting corpses in an anatomy laboratory and in his interviews acted and talked like a "dead" man. He also had dreams in which death had reunited him with his wife, although he did not believe in an afterlife.

The other patient was 48 years old and had a similar reaction when his first wife left him after a marriage of 25 years. Although he had remarried for reasons of convenience, his depression was clearly connected with his first wife. He gave a rather distorted picture of the difficulties in the first marriage, placing all the blame on his wife and minimizing his own drinking. According to his daughter's report he had been active and interested in the family when he was sober. Under the influence of alcohol, however, he was given to rages and often beat her as well as his wife. In a later interview the patient confirmed his daughter's story, and one of his dreams was distinguished by the fact that his first wife was beating him. He accepted this treatment as deserved punishment which would assure him of being forgiven.

He had attempted to electrocute himself with 20,000 volts and sustained severe burns which had kept him in the hospital for a year. His surgeons reported that his mood was worsening as his surgical condition improved. Talking to him, it was clear that this was the case. Never have I seen a man so determined to die. One time when in a slightly better mood and after he discussed with me the possibility of making an effort to recover, he dreamt that he was kidnaped by Hitler's men and taken to a work-shop. He had to work but he could not. In the next part of the dream he was visiting me on my ward and he was in a group that was marching. He heard a voice giving directions and the group was told to eat strawberries and pills.

In his associations he stressed that he liked to eat strawberries, but that his teeth were no longer good enough to chew them. He even regarded the attempt to encourage him to recover as Hitlerian cruelty that called for an effort which he did not wish to make.

The patient died, apparently because he had no desire to live. A week before his death he dreamt that he had jumped from the 47th floor of a building. He then was 48 years old, but he had been one year younger when he made his suicide attempt.

While in these two patients affective deadness was intimately connected with their suicide attempts, this deadness stemmed from a depression precipitated by abandonment. Affective incapacity had not been a primary complaint nor could it be considered a cause of their marital difficulties. In direct contrast to the Swedish patients, few Norwegian spouses made such complaints about each other, although some Norwegian women complained that their husbands were not emotionally demonstrative. When such complaints were heard in Norway, they were usually related to the man's lack of tenderness or to the woman's desire to receive verbal assurances that she was desirable. Where there was poor communication, it was usually the consequence of other problems in the relationship rather than due to basic defects in affectivity.

Many Norwegian women complained that their husbands were rigid or emotionally inflexible. However, this lack of flexibility seemed to characterize both sexes. Some of the nurses expressed the feeling that being too easily influenced by others was one of their most serious faults. Their stories indicated, however, that they were far from compliant and merely reproached themselves for those rare occasions when they had been willing to be persuaded by others to change a decision or to alter a plan. Unwittingly, they regarded flexibility as a weakness, and it was less respected than rigidity. The previously discussed tendency of the Norwegians to hold on to their anger was in some ways but another example of this rigidity.

In the most paranoid patients their openly expressed anger complicated the establishment of a personal contact with them. At times they either refused to talk or abruptly broke off their interviews. Some could be persuaded to be less guarded at least temporarily. One paranoid young boy came to his sessions with his arms crossed over his chest and with an angry expression on his face. During the interview it was observed that his arms went to his side and his face softened while he talked relatively freely. As soon as the session was over, his arms and facial expression returned to their original position. In general, Norwegian faces were strikingly more expressive than those of Swedes and rarely showed the Swedish mask-like quality.

In Norway psychiatric work with patients was facilitated by their emotional capacity once a relationship had been established with them. However, these patients presented other problems that had to be dealt with before they became amenable to a meaningful contact. Five of them promised and even seemed eager to come back as outpatients, but I soon learned not to take such promises too seriously. They failed to show up for appointments unless they were each time reminded of my continued interest. The Norwegian patients seemed inclined to consider both the doctor and the hospital as authorities to be circumvented, and they were untruthful without feelings of guilt. This behavior differed from that of Swedish patients, who usually treated a doctor deferentially. In any case, they kept their appointments or telephoned when they were unable to do so.

Norwegian male patients were more likely than those in Denmark or Sweden to give false information in order to protect their egos, especially if they had been left by their girlfriends or wives. For example, one man, who had broken his engagement, tearfully begged his fiancée to take him back. He told his friends that it was his fiancée who came crying to him and requested reconciliation. When caught in a lie the patient would sheepishly admit the truth rather than become guilty or angry.

Actually such incidents led in several cases to the establishment of a satisfactory contact with the patient.

While Norwegian patients clearly differed from their Danish and Swedish counterparts in their ability to express anger, they resembled the Danes in their ability to laugh at themselves and in their ability to cry openly. There was not a single Swedish male patient who cried during the interviews, while such incidents did occur in Norwegian and Danish male patients.

Half of the nurses and patients came from homes where affection between parents and children was not openly expressed, and many of them had the same difficulty. Of course, these families varied widely in the extent to which interest and emotion were otherwise communicated, and these alternative patterns undoubtedly played a significant role. The emotional life of Norwegians coming from such backgrounds is protected by other factors than simply their ability to express anger and dissatisfaction. Norwegian children are not expected to be as emotionally controlled as Swedish children, nor as well behaved as either Swedish or Danish children. Nor must they be as neat, clean and well dressed as children in Sweden or Denmark. They are also more outgoing than Danish or Swedish children as evidenced by the fact that young children (aged 4 to 10) in my building or at the local tennis court took the initiative in approaching and questioning me. In Sweden and Denmark the children waited to talk until they were spoken to.

Norwegian boys are permitted to cry more readily than are boys in Sweden, and they will do so when angry or frustrated. If they are spanked or hurt themselves, they make an effort to be manly and not to cry. Girls, of course, are less restrained. Both sexes are free to express excitement and joy. After the age of 12 or 13 the demand for emotional control increases in both sexes.

Girls in Norway, as elsewhere, are expected to be emotionally mature at an earlier age than boys. They are supposed to show consideration for their mothers and learn to be protective by caring for young children and animals, from kittens to calves, as a kind of preparation for their role as mothers.

When grown up, girls as well as boys—but especially the former—are expected to be outwardly modest. It was noted in an earlier chapter that in response to the question "Are you a good nurse?" not one Norwegian nurse answered unequivocally in the affirmative—all said that they were about average. By contrast, 11 of the 12 American nurses questioned in the same manner did not hesitate to say yes. This difference was not an indication of greater confidence on the part of the American group, but rather reflected the modesty expected of the Norwegian girl.

In summary, while the Norwegian patients were at times as reserved as the Swedish patients, they usually enjoyed greater affective freedom than the latter. Individual suicidal patients in Norway complained about emotional deadness in the same manner as in Sweden, but as a group they did not show that generalized form of affective deadness observed in Sweden, particularly among male patients. Compared to the Swedish groups, non-suicidal patients and non-patients in Norway also showed greater emotional freedom, and it has been indicated in previous chapters that emotional deadness or the feeling of being already dead are fertile soil for suicidal ideas. By avoiding the widespread affectivity problems of the Swedes, the Norwegians seem to escape a major aspect of the greater Swedish proneness to suicide.

                    ❋   ❋   ❋

What about the Norwegian attitudes toward success and performance—factors that played such an important role in the problem of suicide in Sweden?

Norwegian patients did not have the dreams of competitive struggle that were characteristic of their Swedish counterparts. However, one dream did occur many times with the Norwegian patients, and it involved their winning small fortunes in the Norwegian *tipping* or money lottery by chance or sometimes through a "system." One man dreamt of winning a car in such a lottery, and several others found money outright in the street. The recurrent theme was that either money or other material wealth was acquired without effort, reminding one of a popular theme in the classic Norwegian folk tales of Asbjørnsen and Moe. Askeladden, the hero of the tales, is an idle dreamer who sits by the fire, in contrast to his hard-working, more realistic brothers. Nevertheless, he acquires wealth, power and a princess as a reward for his goodness of heart.*

There were, indeed, indications that thoughts associated with too much success aroused anxiety because the envy and hostility of others were fearfully anticipated or the idea of personal success conflicted with dependency wishes, the nature of which has already been discussed. As to the anticipated fears, they were not totally irrational, because the general attitude is to envy and belittle anyone who stands out too much or is too successful.

The following two cases illustrate some of the fears and anxieties aroused by success and their connection with the patient's dependency problems.

The patient was a 40 year old man who started as a small wholesaler in ceramic articles and built this business into a successful enterprise. He had been married for 13 years and had two children. Three years before the patient's suicide attempt his father-in-law died and his mother-in-law began to spend much of her time in her daughter's home. He complained about her influence over his wife, and these complaints were usually concerned with decisions as to how money was to be spent. His mother-in-law had even advised his wife to ask to be paid for helping him in the business. He wanted his wife to take a stand against her mother and to ask her to leave. He did not think that he himself should do it, remarking sheepishly, "What can

---

* In Norway, the response of male patients to the first picture on the TAT, which shows a boy sitting in front of a violin, revealed an interesting difference from the Swedish response. The stories that patients are to make up using this picture as a stimulus tend to disclose their aspirations and ambitions as well as the ways in which they expect to fulfill them. In some Norwegian stories the patient let the boy have a daydream of being a great maestro, but the events usually remained on the level of pleasurable daydreaming. More frequently it was said that the boy did not want to and would not play the violin. There was a strong inclination not to accept the violin as a challenge to be mastered. The Swedish patients seldom rejected this challenge. They considered at once how much hard work and practice would have to go into the boy's effort to become a fine violinist. There were almost no Swedish responses indicating pleasure derived from the playing, a theme which was mentioned in some of the Norwegian stories. Whether the boy succeeded or not, Swedish patients placed the emphasis on translating any fantasies about success into the hard work that was required for achievement.

you say to your wife's mother?" He felt abused by his mother-in-law, but denied that there was any dissatisfaction with his wife. Yet he had not lived at home for six months, leaving his wife and two children as well as his mother-in-law.

Eventually a different picture of his marital situation emerged. He criticized his wife for spending most of her time in women's clubs. She neither read books not did she wish to discuss anything with him. She was an extravagant spender and refused to keep a household budget. She had no interest in his business and did not want to hear about his problems. Although he was angry at his wife in many areas, he justified this anger through his mother-in-law's role in the home, and chose to feel *forurettet* in that situation. Before his suicide attempt he wrote in a note to his mother that his mother-in-law was to blame for his death. When he moved out of his house, he took an apartment and asked his mother to keep house for him. Since he had been a heavy drinker for 12 years, his wife actually wanted him to leave unless he stopped drinking.

While in the hospital the patient had the following dream: he was infatuated with a woman and helping her in her business.

He complained about his business and the continual anxieties connected with it. He resented the unpleasant expressions of envy from his friends that his financial success had aroused. His wife and mother-in-law knew that he was making money and thought that they could spend as much as they wanted to. His own mother had helped him in his business and was managing the firm while he was in the hospital. She had had some business experience and was quite competent, so that he assumed that the woman in the dream was his mother. Apart from expressing his emotional tie to her, he reversed their roles by becoming her helper. He also indicated that he wanted to sell his business and work for someone else in order to get rid of his anxieties and responsibilities. Presenting a lottery ticket, he stated that if he should win 75,000 kroner he would sell his business at once.

Prior to his suicide attempt the patient did everything to ruin his business, and in doing so there was a strong element of spite toward his wife and her mother. Success in business had also taken him too far away from his dependency cravings, and even his complaint that his wife lacked interest in the business became understandable in that light. While he believed that his success had brought his wife's mother into the home and had drawn both women closer together, his difficulties partly served the purpose of bringing his own mother closer to him.

The second case was that of a 36 year old married man who was one of the non-suicidal patients. He complained that his father did not give him enough responsibility in their fairly large business. He described his father as a man who always had to be on top whether in conversation or business. Although the patient was less ambitious, he did want to make some of the decisions in the business, and he even thought that he could run it alone. He also complained that he had never been close to his father and stressed that he had given far more companionship to his own son than he had ever received from his father. In many of his dreams he found himself in a high place with only a railing for support, frightened by the possibility of falling. His associations revealed that he was afraid to take over the business or to be given such a high position in the firm that he would no longer be able to depend on his father for support.

These two patients were unusual since for most Norwegian patients success and achievement were not major preoccupations. The Norwegian men clearly differed in this respect from the Swedes. For patients such as these two, imaginary success was not satisfactory and real success was a major threat. Their histories were unique, but similar to each other in that both grew up in families that were dominated by a strong parent who overvalued performance and achievement in the upbringing of children.

The majority of Norwegian patients were not pressured by a particularly successful or ambitious father (or mother) in the direction of great achievement. The previously described obsessional type of father could be exacting toward his children, but was ritualistic in the expectation of good or obedient behavior rather than outstanding performance. Consequently, when obsessional working habits were observed in adult patients, they differed from those in the United States in that they were not based on great ambition for success. The main concern of the obsessional Norwegian is centered around some equivalent of being "good" and in deriving a feeling of security from this good behavior.

The Norwegian child is not required to excel in order to win his mother's affection. The mother is usually the dominant force in shaping the child's character, and she encourages his claim to omnipotence without insisting on proof that it has been earned. Norwegian boys are not expected as they are in Sweden to excel under any circumstances. They please their mothers by being good, and good behavior means that they cause no trouble either in school or later in life.

It is thus not so surprising that Norwegian adults do not drive themselves toward success or develop the degree of self-hatred if they fail, that was seen in the Swedes. They are inclined to deal with failure by rationalization without self-blame, or by blaming others and remaining omnipotent at least in fantasy. Alcohol seems to help them in maintaining such fantasies, but the Norwegians have less need for suicide as a self-punishment for failure—a mechanism that plays such an important role in the high Swedish suicide rate.

The Norwegian tendency to be content with fantasy rather than to insist on success in reality is well described in the plays of Ibsen.[8] *Peer Gynt's* point of departure is one of the Asbjørnsen and Moe tales with the omnipotent dreamer as the typical Norwegian theme. Although Peer's mother lives to regret his grandiosity, she has in earlier years encouraged it. In fact, from the opening *"Peer, du lyver"* (Peer, you lie) to the touchingly perceptive scene in which Åse lies dying and she and Peer take their imaginary sleigh ride, Åse and Peer embody much of what is significant and characteristic in the Norwegian mother-son relationship. Åse's death is followed by a series of unrealistic fantasies of omnipotent success, extending from Peer as tycoon to Peer as prophet. Peer eventually fails, but he does not judge himself harshly, and he is fighting death at the play's end. A suicide Peer would never be. As a study in "national character," it would be hard to find a rival for *Peer Gynt* in the literature of any country.

As the antithesis of Peer, Brand is the model of what the Norwegian should be. His motto of "all or nothing" amounts to a choice between success or suicide. In the inflexible and uncompromising pursuit of his moral and religious goals he destroys his wife, his child and himself.

The conflict between Brand's attitude and Peer's is typical of Ibsen's work, with characters representing the different attitudes often contrasted in the same play. In *The Wild Duck*, Gregers is the uncompromising figure. He insists that his friend Ekdal be stripped of his illusions, which include his duck, his fantasy of an invention that will make him wealthy and solve his financial problems, and his misconceptions about his marriage. Ekdal is disillusioned, and his love for his wife and 13 year old daughter, Hedvig, is destroyed in the process. Rejected by her father, Hedvig kills herself, her death symbolizing a murder of love by Greger's Brandian outlook.

John Gabriel Borkman was in love with a woman whom he unscrupulously deserted for the conquest of the business world. He succeeded, then failed and lived in the hope of reconquest. When he loses that hope, he commits suicide. On the Peer side of the coin is his friend Foldal, for whom life is always possible because he can find consolation in his dreams and wishful thoughts.

In fact, although suicide is relatively infrequent in Norway, it often occurs in Ibsen's plays where those committing it are the persons with Brand's outlook. Professor Rubek (*When We Dead Awaken*) is in the world of sculpture what Brand is in religion and Borkman in business. His love for Irene is sacrificed for the pursuit of artistic success. Rosmer and Rebecca (*Rosmersholm*) prefer death to an imperfect love, and the pregnant Hedda Gabler kills herself when her concepts of love and motherhood become irreconcilable.

Ibsen did not hesitate in his plays to romanticize and glorify the willingness to die rather than compromise. He stated in a letter that "Brand is myself in my best moments." It is clear that he saw Peer as representing most of the Norwegian people most of the time. Intellectually, he appears to be advocating an attitude that refuses to compromise with principle even if it means suicide. One is compelled to regard his solution as intellectually conceived, for in the last analysis, in Brand he had created a very unlovable figure, and in Peer a most lovable one.

However, in ridiculing the Ekdals and Peers, Ibsen is aware of the anxieties aroused by Brand's attitude in those Norwegians who adopt it. "All or nothing" may lead to great success, but such success can be dangerous and tends to be followed by an even greater fall (*Brand, Borkman, The Master Builder*).

The Master Builder epitomizes both the conquest of success and the fear aroused by it, symbolized by Ibsen—and some of the Norwegian patients—as a fear of heights. In climbing the church steeple and defying his fear, Solness falls to his death, which in a sense is also a suicide.

✿   ✿   ✿

Like the Danes and Swedes, the Norwegians have a Lutheran church which is affiliated with the State. Of the 12 Norwegian nurses eight expressed a belief in God and seven in an afterlife. Of the 25 suicidal patients, 20 believed in God, with a majority (15) affirming their belief in an afterlife, while the other five were unsure about it. Only a few patients expected suicide to be punished in an afterlife. This special group was of particular clinical interest, because the patients came from very religious families and belonged to an important minority whose suicidal pattern was strongly influenced by the pietistic attitudes and moral traditions of rural Norway.

A 32 year old unmarried woman, addicted to morphine and barbiturates for ten years, was admitted to the hospital after she had taken a large overdose of both drugs. She claimed that she had not intended to die. She merely wanted to get away from her troubles, although she had thought that perhaps she might never wake up. Her recent life had been a nightmare of drugs, arrests, hospitalizations, and fears of being detected by the police. She was guarded and evasive in her interviews and failed to tell more than half-truths. She later admitted that this habit had become so ingrained that she had difficulty in telling the truth even when she wanted to. In view of her additional overindulgence in alcohol and marked promiscuity, one was tempted to classify her simply as a psychopath. However, her story proved to be more complicated.

She came from a family of seven children in western Norway and she had a non-identical twin sister. Her parents, and particularly her mother, belonged to a fundamentalist sect which strictly prohibits almost all pleasure, from sex to smoking. When the patient dated a boy regularly in her teens, she did it secretly because of her family's beliefs. Secretiveness became part of a general pattern of not confiding in her parents, while her twin sister was much more outgoing and not afraid of disclosing most of the things that happened in her life.

At the age of 14 and under the influence of a religious revival which swept the town near the end of World War II, the patient bowed to her parents' religious convictions and became an active church member. While she first joined the revival movement to please her mother, it eventually became her way of life. When she was 18 years old, she became a member of a particular church group (*menighet*) and strictly applied its codes to her own life.

However, when she reached the age of 22 this pattern broke wide open. She decided one night to drink in order to see what alcohol was like. She became intoxicated and went on a spree that was known to everyone in her small home town. Her church group decided to discipline her by suspending her from certain church activities for a year. While on probation she rebelled bitterly against this punishment and became particularly resentful of her group leader, who had been fond of her and should have defended her. (Years later she revenged herself on this man by inducing him to invite her to his hotel room while on a trip to Oslo without his wife. When he was already undressed and sexually aroused, she refused him and reminded him of the old incident.) Her addiction to barbiturates began with her inability to sleep after she had been publicly punished by her church group. Soon thereafter she had her first sexual affair, and lost an important prop through the marriage of her twin sister. Her need for pills increased, and she proceeded to the use of morphine.

During this period the patient made her first suicide attempt. She knew that her mother, who had recently had a severe heart attack, had been informed about her drinking episode. She was afraid that her mother would die and that she would be the cause. She resolved not to live after her mother's death, but then did not wait for this event. She lay down in the snow and fell asleep. Upon awakening she changed her mind and was willing to find out whether her mother would recover. The mother did recover and was still alive many years later.

Despite anger and bitterness toward her sectarian group, the patient did not break with the church as a whole. She main-

tained her parents' beliefs, although she no longer felt strong
enough to follow them. She managed during her irregular home
visits to hide her drug addiction from her parents and was even
afraid to smoke in their presence because she wanted them to
think of her as a good Christian. She believed in both an afterlife and a reunion of good Christians after death and was convinced that all others "were damned and would be punished."
She was able to quote the Bible by heart when necessary to
prove the validity of her religious beliefs.

The patient's dreams indicated that her promiscuity served
the dual purpose of defying her father and punishing herself
masochistically for doing so. This acknowledgment led her to
reveal that misbehavior was the only method of obtaining
attention from her father, who usually favored the other twin.
Her underlying wish was for him to discover her behavior so
that he would take an interest in protecting her. She treated
her interviews in a similar manner, gradually confessing misdeeds
and misadventures after first making a big secret of them.

The history of another patient, who was mentioned in the
chapter dealing with the psychodynamics of suicide, is particularly relevant in the present context. He was a 30 year old
seaman from Finnmark, whose father was a fisherman and
frequently away from home. Nevertheless, the patient felt
closer to him than to his mother, a nervous and irritable woman
who was partial to his two older brothers. She was a Baptist
and a *personlig kristen* (meaning someone who in his personal
life acts in accord with his religious beliefs). She did not for-
bid drinking and smoking, but created the impression in the
patient that a good Christian would do neither. She also was a
strict disciplinarian and frequently beat him. Although he bitterly resented these beatings, he never showed any sign of pain
and he came to disrespect his mother because of her inability to
control her temper. As the sixth of eight children, he grew up
with the feeling that he was "superfluous" in the family. At the
age of 18 he left to become a seaman, and this was the time
when according to his report he began to feel depressed and to
drink excessively. When he was 25 years old, he married a girl
who was critical of everything he did, while she admired her
father, so that here too the patient felt superfluous. She refused
to move with him when he found a small apartment, and his

drinking habits led to frequent fights, followed by divorce within three years.

For a while the patient continued to work as a seaman, but he had frequent fights aboard ship and while in port. Having finally been blacklisted as a seaman, he was unable to continue this work, became more and more depressed, and impulsively attempted to commit suicide by leaping in front of a car.

Significantly, the first part of the patient's dream in connection with his suicide attempt dealt with an exploding atom bomb, and the second with his being in hell about to be burnt while his brother looked on in approval. His associations indicated that hell was a punishment he expected and deserved for his aggression toward his siblings, his explosive temper and his un-Christian life.

He had made other suicide attempts in an impulsive manner. Once he had tried to jump into a ship's propeller; on another occasion he was severely injured when he jumped in front of a jeep; and he also attempted once to drown himself. All his earlier attempts were explained by him as having been precipitated by unfair discipline following his fights, while the last one was ascribed to his inability to obtain fair treatment in the form of a job on a ship.

The patient remained in contact with his family and returned home for several months at a time, only to become restless again and leave. Similarly, he sometimes was an active member of his church, but these quiet periods alternated with episodes of fighting and drinking, during which he reproached himself for violating his mother's religious beliefs. He had frequent dreams in which he begged various people to forgive him.

For a time one could only surmise the anger toward his mother that underlay his anger toward the world. Eventually it became more evident. In one of his dreams he was in the company of a detective, searching for two female criminals. When they were found, one received a mild prison sentence, while he forgave the other woman and then married her. With the interviewer acting as the detective, the woman who was sentenced to prison was his former wife, whom he hated bitterly and previously wanted to kill. His mother was the woman who was forgiven and then became his wife, and his dream clearly reflected his mixed feelings, namely, resentment at having been mistreated by her and yet yearning for her love. He forgave her, much as he wished that she would forgive him. The general tone of leniency in the dream was in keeping with the fact that he no longer was acutely depressed and was now more lenient with himself. The dream sequence of crime—forgiveness—closeness may have been a reflection of the fact that the patient's troubles began when offenses against good behavior seemed to him to be the best method of winning the attention and affection of his puritanical mother.

This seaman as well as the female addict viewed suicide as a self-punishment for sin. After death the non-sinful would be reunited with loved ones, while the sinful were damned and would continue to be punished. Both patients considered that they deserved the damnation and punishment they expected to receive. While suicide was a self-punishment, it was itself a sin and served as further evidence of their sinfulness.

The pietistic suicidal patients with their alternating antisocial behavior and religious conformity had a distinctly Norwegian character. Patients from pietistic families were seen in Sweden and Denmark, but the characterological impact on such patients seemed to be nowhere as great as in Norway and certainly played a less important role in the causation of suicide.

While these two Norwegian patients were caught in a painful conflict between aggression and conscience, not every suicidal patient who lived an antisocial existence and came from a religious background was the genuine victim of such a conflict. In another patient who went from alcoholism and robbery to abstinence, hard work and religiosity, both his church activity and his suicide attempt were merely designed to persuade others that he was penitent, since he knew that this reaction was expected of him.

The "life is duty, suffering is ennobling, pleasure is corrupting" attitude encountered in some areas of rural Norway did not always have a religious cast. One patient grew up in a brutally enforced work-without-fun routine from early childhood, but religion was neither given as the reason nor used to enforce this code. What seemed crucial for those coming from a formally religious family was not religion as such, but the extent to which its application was accompanied by warmth and affection at home. Where this was not the case, a combination of duty and religion was all that parents could give their children. Four of the 12 Norwegian nurses came from pietistic families. One appeared to be so affected by it that at the age of 35 she still rejected all interested men on account of their religious inadequacies. Another broke away from her family's pietistic way of life, but not completely and not without feelings of guilt. A third seemed to conform to her parents' beliefs, and although she did not have much pleasure, she lived without acute suffering. A fourth nurse had softened parental beliefs and customs into something she could more comfortably live with. This strict puritanical background in both patients and non-patients is a remnant of a far more puritanical era in rural Norway; the pattern was not seen among those who had been born and brought up in Oslo.

The Norwegian attitude toward alcoholism is partly a reaction to a genuine problem and partly a carryover from the puritanical tradition of the country. Excessive drinking is considered an important social problem in all three Scandinavian countries, as it is in the United States. However, the Norwegians' attitude is more moralistic than that of Swedes or Danes. "Alcoholic" has a pejorative implication in Norway that cannot be compared with anything in the United States or the rest of Scandinavia. Consequently Norwegian patients are ashamed of their drinking and will minimize it, cover it up, or lie about it to an unusual extent.

Physicians maintained the same attitude toward alcoholics as did the general public, showing either a lack of interest in their treatment, or considerable irritation or contempt. Equally characteristic was the attitude of the Norwegian nurses, several of whom, in response to a question as to what qualities they desired in an ideal man, stated spontaneously that he should *not* be an alcoholic—a response that while it seemed amusing reflected the Norwegian problem and preoccupation with drinking.

There were many blind spots in the Norwegian concern with alcoholism. Marital conflicts were apt to be drowned in alcohol and many of the male patients, if moderate drinkers before marriage, became excessive drinkers afterwards. Wives often considered their husbands as adequate apart from their drinking, and husbands as well as wives seemed to focus on alcoholism as a way of avoiding their underlying difficulties. A somewhat different emphasis in psychiatric diagnosis should be noted here: in Norway, if alcoholism is part of the clinical picture, it will generally be listed as the main psychiatric diagnosis, while in a similar case in the United States, Sweden or Denmark, it would probably be listed as a subordinate symptom under various other diagnoses. Here again, professional attitudes may reflect those prevailing in the population as a whole.

Shame and disgrace are not attached to suicide to nearly the same extent as they are to alcoholism. Some of the patients expressed concern about the possibility that others might hear of their suicide attempt. One of them refused to see people until the scars on his wrist had healed. A few other patients expressed the hope that either their wives' relatives or their employers would not be informed about their suicide attempt. Several patients from pietistic families felt ashamed because they expected their relatives to be troubled by their behavior, but the act of suicide was not what they were really concerned about. On the whole, suicidal patients in Norway showed perhaps a little more shame than the Danes, and somewhat less than the Swedes.

One of the signs of shame, which was rarely observed in Norwegian patients, involved the effort to cover up or minimize the suicide attempt. In Sweden many male patients shamefully equated suicide with weakness and felt compelled to minimize it. In Norway such an effort to cover up was observed mainly with regard to drinking. The Norwegian nurses, too, showed a good deal of sympathy for suicidal patients—perhaps not surprising for nurses—but they were often much harsher and less tolerant toward alcoholic patients.

At the time of this study people in Oslo were much concerned about the fact that several young men committed or attempted to commit suicide in prison while awaiting trial. In interviewing one of these men it was established that his suicide attempt had been more manipulative than serious. Nevertheless, since other patients made genuine suicide attempts in the aftermath of criminal behavior, a few comments about this problem may be in order.

For patients in this group, prison and the shame brought upon them by public and parental knowledge regarding their misdeeds amount to extreme humiliation. In Norway, as was pointed out before, to be good (*snill*) is the basic rule for children, and this rule means first and foremost not to get into any trouble. Then too, whether confinement serves punitive or psychiatric purposes, it is likely to be more difficult for Norwegians than for most people. Great value is placed on the individual right to move about freely, and this Norwegian trait is anchored in a tradition that goes back to Viking days and has seen the Norwegian as immigrant, pioneer, explorer, fisherman, mountain climber and wanderer. "I'm a free man in a free country and can go where I please" were the words of one patient, and they were said with satisfaction and pride rather than belligerence. Depriving the Norwegian of this freedom to go where he pleases is bound to take from him an adaptive tool that is very much a part of his character.*

❁   ❁   ❁

It may be helpful to bring together the factors in the character of Norwegians which appear to make them less prone to suicide than the Swedes or Danes. At the same time an attempt will be made to summarize those characteristics playing an essential role in Norwegians who are suicidal.

---

* Schiødt[9] contends that a high Norwegian emigration rate is a major factor in the low Norwegian suicide rate. The emigrants are presumably dissatisfied people who, if they stayed home, might have been the suicides of Norway, and they either solve their problems by emigrating or instead become the suicides of countries such as the United States. The high Danish suicide rate would then be explained by a low Danish emigration rate. Schiødt points to an inverse relationship in the fluctuations of the Danish emigration and suicide rates as evidence for his thesis.

This hypothesis is difficult to uphold for many reasons. The Norwegian suicide rate has been consistently low regardless of great fluctuations in the Norwegian emigration rate. Since 1930 Norwegian emigration has fallen off to a rate below the Danish, without a significant rise in the Norwegian suicide rate. A United States Public Health Service study done in 1960 throws further light on this subject. It showed that for the year of 1959 there were 37 suicides among Americans born in Norway and 39 suicides among Americans born in Denmark. The total Norwegian born population of the United States is twice the Danish born population, so that even in the United States the "Danish rate" was twice the "Norwegian." Even more importantly, Schiødt's hypothesis disregards the basic character differences evidenced by the Norwegian's historical tendency to move if he is dissatisfied and the Dane's preference for remaining where he is.

While the Norwegian mother-child relationship has some similarities to the Danish, there are important differences. An independent, self-sufficient child is highly valued in Norway (as he is in Sweden) and the child's personal freedom is not likely to be restricted. The focusing of the mother's emotional life on the child is to some extent counterbalanced by this desire for an independent child. Conversely, the child's self-sufficiency does not indicate a real lack of emotional involvement on the part of the mother as it often does in Sweden. In Norwegian patients who were suicidal, this counterbalancing may have failed in either direction. However, Norwegians are unlikely in adulthood to be as dependent in their adaptation as are the Danes and, what is more, they are not as vulnerable to a loss of dependency gratification.

Norwegian women are inclined to inject their own dependency longings into the relationship with their children. Significantly, therefore, younger women who attempt to commit suicide are especially those whose own dependency frustrations have reached a point where they did not want to care for their children altogether.

As to the frequency of reunion-after-death fantasies and a rather lenient attitude toward suicide (considered as an act that would be forgiven and not prevent one's happy afterlife), the Norwegian patients (excepting the pietistic group) were found to resemble the Danish patients. In Norway, however, one does not see those extremely rapid funerals with a brief period of mourning and a general "get it over quickly" attitude toward death, which are common in Denmark and apparently reflect the widespread separation anxieties of the Danes.

Furthermore, arousing the child's guilt is not the major method of discipline in Norway that it is in Denmark. Neither Norwegian men nor women tend to arouse guilt or sympathy as the best means of gaining attention or forcing affection, and the use of suicide as a form of emotional blackmail is much rarer in Norway than in Denmark.

Also, Norwegian women are not as insecure and preoccupied with the necessity of holding their men as Swedish women are, nor are they as vulnerable to the loss of a man as are women in Sweden or Denmark. If an older Norwegian woman is suicidal, she is more likely to be vulnerable to the loss of, or the permanent separation from, her adult children. However, there are relatively few women who carry a close relationship with their children to such an extreme.

Norwegian children as well as adults have their characteristic ways of handling anger and being *forurettet*. There is a tendency to paranoid pathology, and the failure of paranoid defenses can lead to depression and suicide; here suicide as an internalized murder may be seen. For Norwegian women with suicidal tendencies, repressed anger directed toward their children is more difficult to handle than that directed toward their men. Every woman is expected to be desirous of caring for her child, and the guilt feelings of those who are unable to do so are correspondingly pronounced. However, regardless of the kind or intensity of anger developed by a Norwegian child or adult, there is far less need here for the repression of anger than is seen in Denmark or in the characteristically detached Swedes. The ability of Norwegians to feel justifiably angry and to express their anger freely precludes the usual retroflexion of anger that was so characteristic of both Danish and Swedish patients and was such an important factor in the suicide problem of those two countries.

Since Norwegian children are not expected to practice that early suppression of emotional expression that is required of the young Swedish child, they are emotionally freer as adults. In escaping the Swedish affectivity problems and related feelings of deadness, the Norwegians avoid that proneness to suicide associated with such feelings.

The pietistic group believes that suicide is sinful and a deserved self-punishment that will continue after death. However, the Norwegian demands for success and achievement are far less rigid than those of Swedish patients. Being first is not required of them by their parents when they are young, nor do they require it of themselves as adults. They may wish to be better, but generally do not have to be best and do not make the strenuous efforts of the Swedish patients to achieve their goals. Lack of achievement does not result in the enormous self-hatred or the great need for self-punishment seen in Swedish patients. The death-as-self-punishment-for-failure fantasies of the Swedes were conspicuous in Norway by their absence.

CHAPTER VII

Conclusions and Applications

AT THE CONCLUSION of the preceding chapter emphasis was placed on the reasons for the low suicide rate in Norway in comparison with the high rates in Sweden and Denmark. Of equal significance in this study has been the finding that the suicide rates in Sweden and Denmark are high for reasons that are quite different. This observation has important implications for the exploration of suicide and of other clinical problems as well, particularly in the context of cross-cultural comparisons.

What is seen in Sweden may be called a "performance" type of suicide. Based on rigid performance expectations with strong self-hatred for failure and set in the matrix of a particular Swedish affectivity problem, such performance suicide is also traceable to an early mother-child separation. Suicides of the performance variety are probably common among the Germans and Swiss and, with important modifications, the Japanese. However, in each of these countries suicide is likely to have its own specific features which are revealing about the culture as a whole and which would make the cross-cultural study of suicide in these countries worthwhile.

In Denmark one encountered primarily a "dependency loss" type of suicide. Specific Danish features are a tendency toward passivity, oversensitivity to abandonment, and an effective use of the technique of arousing guilt in others; once again, these features have their basis in Danish family patterns. The "dependency loss" or "love" type of suicide committed by Danish men and, to a lesser degree, by Norwegian men seems almost a romantic anachronism, since performance suicides are apparently becoming more and more the rule in our modern world.

Norway also served as an experimental laboratory for another type of suicide which is best described as a "moral" form of suicide. It stems from aggressive antisocial behavior and strong guilt feelings aroused by such behavior, with the entire constellation cast in a puritanical setting.

Since the United States is a nation of various subcultures, it is not surprising that elements of all three suicidal patterns are also encountered here. However, because of the multiplicity and innumerable mixtures of patterns in this country, the task of identifying the various psychodynamic patterns of suicide here is an extremely difficult one. Hence the opportunity of observing these patterns in a "purer" form and under their original formative conditions is comparable to having a vast clinical laboratory in which thorough studies of the psychodynamics of suicide* can be conducted.

After a study of suicide in Scandinavia, the "dependency loss," "performance," and "moral" types of suicide, as we see them in the United States, could not only be more clearly defined, but critical factors distinguishing the psychodynamics of each type, such as differing attitudes toward death and various fantasies about an afterlife, could be identified and made meaningful. By limiting the variables one must deal with, the study of suicide in the more homogeneous Scandinavian cultures simplifies the separation of the psychodynamic factors that are essential from those that are superfluous.

In fact, such a "cross-cultural laboratory" would probably prove equally productive in the study of other clinical entities. After all, the number of ways in which individual and social maladjustment may be expressed is clearly limited: suicide, neurosis, crime, alcoholism, and a few other conditions. It is reasonable to assume that these entities vary qualitatively, i.e., in meaning and significance, as well as quantitatively from country to country.

---

* The lack of interest in psychodynamic studies of psychosocial problems in Scandinavia has partly been due to the fact that psychoanalysis is cut off from the mainstream of psychiatry in a way that has had harmful effects on both disciplines. Clinical studies of suicide in all three countries have largely been statistical rather than motivational in approach, i.e., they have dealt with variations in age, sex, method, social situation and clinical diagnosis of large samples of attempted suicides. Psychodynamic ideas regarding suicide are usually summarized for the sake of completeness. My work on suicide began with such a statistical-psychiatric study, and it is certain that many of these Scandinavian studies have been competently and diligently conducted.[1] However, the point of diminishing returns has long since been reached in such work, so that these studies have essentially become confirmations of each other.

Depression, for example, has a different form of clinical expression in Sweden from that found in Denmark. More common in Sweden is an anxiety type of depression in which the individual redoubles his activity with diminishing effectiveness. This symptomatology seems to be the result of a combination of an early mother-child separation and the young child's learning to use his performance as a means of winning parental affection. In Denmark dependency is encouraged to a later age, based on the suppression of aggression rather than on performance. Hence the classical depressive picture with diminished activity and a yearning for maternal care predominates.

Obsessional behavior, to take another example, usually arises from obedience-defiance conflicts. However, if such conflicts occur under conditions which are characterized by the need for high achievement, as they often are in the United States and Sweden, or by demands for being good, as in Norway, entirely different personality features come to the foreground.

Even in Western cultures, a character trait as well as a clinical syndrome may vary in psychodynamic significance from culture to culture. With some justification the Swede has been called "ambitious" or "industrious" in the usual descriptions of his national character. However, as has been indicated in the course of this study, these traits have a particular meaning for the Swede, since they are related to a very early maternal separation and an emphasis on competitive performance as a way of repairing self-esteem and winning parental love and affection. Moreover, industriousness as a character trait has long been attributed to the Germans, the Swiss and the Japanese. The available evidence indicates that the trait has a rather different psychodynamic structure in those peoples from that seen in Sweden. Thus even when a character description is superficially correct, its significance is not clear unless its psychological meaning is known.

Even the psychological defense mechanisms available to us, i.e., repression, projection, detachment, etc., are limited in number and probably universal in use. A given culture can also encourage a preference for one or another mechanism in the handling of emotional conflict. The Swedish preference for detachment in the management of emotions in general and of anger in particular exemplifies this process of selection.

In recent years much attention has been paid to the possibility that male homosexuality may be as valuable a barometer for psychosocial tension and pressure as are crime, suicide and alcoholism. In this connection the question has often been raised whether male homosexuality is as severe a problem in the Scandinavian countries as it is in other parts of western Europe and the United States. Unfortunately no adequate technique for estimating the frequency of male homosexuality has as yet been established. Kinsey[2] concluded that 20th century figures for male homosexuality have remained constant in the United States, while many American psychoanalysts familiar with the problem have expressed the belief that there has been a marked increase during the past 20 years. It would probably not be too difficult to develop adequate techniques for estimating the incidence of both male homosexuality and alcoholism (see the chapter on Norway), if a joint psychiatric, sociologic and statistical effort were made. It is regrettable that no group investigation of this kind has been undertaken as yet.

While it was impossible in the frame of this study to estimate the frequency of male homosexuality in the Scandinavian countries, it may be of interest to note that it was only in the Danish sample that either overt homosexuality or anxieties connected with homosexual behavior were encountered with any frequency. One suicidal patient in the Danish group was overtly homosexual. A second had a homosexual brother, whose suicide was ascribed to unhappiness caused by his sexual deviation. Another man was afraid of being regarded as effeminate by others. A female patient was concerned about her husband's infrequent sexual desire and general effeminate appearance, and expressed the belief that he might be homosexual. However, such incidents were not more common in this series of Danish patients than would be expected in a comparable American sample.

In fact, overt homosexuality or the fear of being homosexual occurred rather infrequently among the Swedish and Norwegian patients, despite my search for both in the two countries. Particularly in Sweden it might be suspected, because of the strong competitive pressures upon the men, the early mother-child separation and deep-seated conflicts between the sexes, that the rate of homosexuality would be high. However, the over-all picture presented by the Swedish male patients, including those who had potency problems or preferred masculine company and had little regard for the female sex, clearly showed that their sexual desires and fantasies remained centered on women. If confirmed by further studies of homosexuality in Scandinavia, this finding would seem to indicate that the passivity shown by Danish male patients tends to be more decisive in determining a homosexual adaptation than Swedish competitiveness or hostility to women. A cross-cultural comparison of homosexuality in the three Scandinavian countries and the United States would certainly be enlightening.

Similar comparative possibilities are offered by a study of subcultures within the United States. Suicide, crime, alcoholism and neurosis also tend to vary among the subcultures of our country, and here, too, the differences are probably qualitative as well as quantitative. Psychiatry has perhaps tended to regard the study of other cultures or subcultures as a special field of social psychiatry, without realizing the opportunities for clinical research inherent in such work. These clinical potentialities should draw the psychiatrist to such work, apart from any contribution he can make to a science of society.

*   *   *

In the early days of psychoanalysis Freud[3] selected material from primitive cultures primarily to validate his psychoanalytic observations and conclusions. He hoped to find, and did find, evidence for the existence of such a phenomenon as the Oedipal complex in societies other than his own. Geza Roheim[4] used and developed Freud's approach to psychoanalytic anthropology. He described his work as "an attempt to explain civilization or culture as a manifestation of Eros." Social institutions were essentially regarded as the fulfillment of unconscious wishes or expressed reaction formations against such wishes, with no balance between the individual's biological needs and society's demands. In Roheim's later writings social institutions became projections of the stages of ontogenetic development.

His view of female infanticide among the Marquesans may

serve as an illustration. Kardiner[5] related it to acute food shortages and the need for population control and then attempted to trace its consequences in Marquesan polygyny, maternal neglect of children, psychosexual attitudes, etc. In Roheim's opinion, Marquesan infanticide must be the result of a reaction against the father's underlying wish to kill his sons and keep his daughters. Hence he never made an attempt to trace its effects on individual and social adaptation.

Research into differences among nations undertaken by contemporary cultural anthropologists was considered by Roheim to be the "democratic counterpart of the Nazi racial doctrine." Nevertheless, he helped stimulate the interest in psychoanalytic anthropology of a generation of anthropologists, of whom Kluckhohn and Mead have probably been the most influential.[6]

Erich Fromm's[7] work has been at the opposite end of the biocultural pole. In formulating his concept of "social character," he insisted on a strict division between the character structure that a society would like its members to have and the methods employed for the purpose of producing it. Since he took no interest in studying the methods, in dealing with modern society he concentrated on describing the character structure needed under modern capitalism and then drew parallels between capitalistic practice and contemporary character attitudes (e.g., "the exploitative orientation," "the marketing orientation"). Psychodynamic exploration of the avenues along which the member of a society learns, experiences and integrates what is expected of him, has played virtually no role in Fromm's work. He has neither utilized case studies, nor been interested in techniques for investigating any of his hypotheses.

If character could be produced as simply and rationally as Fromm implies, there would not be much need to study it psychodynamically. Even if it were, the particular methods chosen are likely to have consequences that are as important as the end itself. By neglecting the process of psychodynamic integration, Fromm has failed to use the one remarkable tool for investigating social pressures which the analyst has and which the sociologist does not have. While social character can be readily observed by everyone, psychosocial character cannot.

It is not surprising that Fromm's perceptive social observations have been of greater interest to sociologists than to psychodynamically oriented anthropologists or to psychoanalysts themselves. It may be noted, however, that Fromm's main "case study," i.e., that of Martin Luther, led to a stimulating analysis of the interplay between Luther's character and the impact of Reformation capitalism in shaping his eventual religious doctrines. Although Fromm's work may be imperfect with respect to contemporary society and the methods of studying it, his leadership in applying social psychology as an adjunct to economic determinism in a historical perspective seems well established.[8]

Freud's instinctual frame of reference even with its later modifications failed to furnish Roheim with an adequate tool for evaluating the impact of varying social institutions on psychosocial character. Fromm's disregard of psychodynamic integration has limited his work in a similar manner, but for different reasons.

A new application of psychoanalysis to the study of society came when Abram Kardiner[9] investigated primitive cultures to determine the role their social institutions play in shaping their people. He demonstrated that study of the individual's conscious and unconscious mental life can determine which social institutions are decisive and how they are integrated in individual character formation. Unfortunately Kardiner's early claim that the Marquesans have no Oedipus complex and the resulting controversy over the "universality" of this phenomenon caused such a furor that important aspects of his work were overlooked.

In his Marquesan study Kardiner relied on an ethnographer's account and a volume of Marquesan legends. In contrast to his subsequent investigation of Alor, he had at his disposal neither the biographies of individual subjects nor their dreams, and without such material no convincing case could be made for the absence of the Oedipus complex. In fact, Roheim detected various Oedipal aspects in the Marquesan myths. However, since maternal neglect of children was the rule among the Marquesans, Roheim was obliged to explain hatred of the mother on the basis of a "negative Oedipus complex."

Kardiner's basic hypothesis that social institutions profoundly influence psychodynamic constellations was not adequately substantiated until his Alorese study. Here he was able to utilize full ethnographic descriptions and biographical data, the dreams of individual Alorese and the results of Rorschach tests. Hence this study and the one undertaken with Ovesey of the American Negro[10] represent his main contributions to the methodology of cross-cultural investigations.

Kardiner had developed the concept of "basic personality" in his work with primitive cultures, and it served to indicate the vast differences seen among them. In order to contrast primitive and Western culture he analyzed James West's study of Plainville and for comparative purposes was willing to accept the basic personality of the Plainville man as typifying Western society. However, West's biographies, sufficient for his own purpose, were insufficient for psychosocial research; they suggest the inadequacies of any substitute for competent psychoanalytic interviews. Of course the Plainville man is not Western man; he is the Midwestern man in the United States. The differences between a Plainville and an Italian farmer may not be as pronounced as those distinguishing either from an Eskimo; the challenging questions are whether or not there are essential differences among modern Western cultures and how they can be ascertained.

It is the author's hope that the foregoing material on Scandinavia will help to demonstrate that such basic integrative differences do exist with respect to psychosocial character and that they can be identified even in three related modern cultures. These three cultures were relatively easy to work with because of their small and homogeneous populations. In attempting to do such work with larger countries it would be necessary to study various subcultures in order to obtain a satisfactory over-all picture.

The key to such differentiation in modern societies lies in the use of a psychoanalytic approach to interviewing to ascertain the pertinent data. Interviewing techniques sufficient for distinguishing primitive cultures from our own or for conducting surveys in a particular culture appear inadequate for the purpose of defining and understanding psychosocial character differences in modern societies.

Language is obviously a vital factor in any psychoanalytic approach. It was previously noted that in Sweden and Norway where English had not been a required second language as long as in Denmark, fluency in both Swedish and Norwegian was required. Moreover, much can be revealed by special words and idioms of a language. Mention has already been made of the significance of *forurettet* (to feel both righteously angry and unjustly abused) in Norwegian and of *tiga ihjäl* (to kill someone through silence) in Swedish.

Scandinavian psychologists and psychiatrists working with children provided an additional source of information concerning the patterns seen in this study. In Denmark, on the basis of observations on adult patients, a tentative outline was made of what parent-child relations would have to be in order to be compatible with the existing adult patterns. When this picture was checked with the findings of a leading Danish child and family psychiatrist, we were pleasantly surprised by the almost complete agreement.* Similar experiences occurred in Sweden and Norway, where the discussion with local colleagues was postponed until a clear enough picture had emerged.

The best source of information for appraising the psychosocial character of a culture is provided by patients and non-patients. If such data are supported by the observations of child psychiatrists, the results of psychological tests and the analysis of

---

* Such comparisons between observed adult behavior and child rearing patterns should be made only if adult subjects furnish us with psychodynamic evidence of a relationship between the two. Erikson[11] provided us with a good example of faulty methodology in this regard. He proceeded from the premise that the Sioux were known to be great warriors, and wanted to relate it to the fact that Sioux children were severely beaten in order to learn nursing behavior without biting. If they became enraged, they were strapped to cradle boards. According to Erikson, "the necessity of suppressing the biting rage contributed to the tribe's always ready ferocity in that this was stored up, channelized and diverted toward prey and enemy."

This kind of methodological error may become almost as dangerous as the ferocity of the Sioux ever was. It is conceivable that Erikson's hypothesis, psychologically dubious as it appears, may be correct, but it was formulated without real evidence. If adult behavior can be ascribed to some particular childhood experience without psychodynamic evidence obtained directly from these adults as a major criterion, then it would be possible to connect virtually every behavior pattern observed in adults with any social institution that may have existed in childhood. Obviously such a procedure would amount to opening Pandora's box.

the culture's pertinent literature (drama, cartoons, folklore and the women's magazine stories), the validity of directly obtained data is enhanced.

Much could probably be gained from employing the principles and techniques utilized in this project in investigations of various subcultures within the United States. Thorough psychodynamic studies of this kind have been limited in number. Most of them merely served to demonstrate what the investigator "knew" to be "true" before he began. While such work may have its merits, the most rewarding findings come from uncovering entirely unexpected variations in behavior and from tracing their derivation. Psychoanalytic interviewing seems sensitive enough to accomplish this goal.

Psychoanalytic studies following in Roheim's path are still being conducted, but they seem to approach a dead end. Erikson's work had been a step toward liberating libidinal theory from some of its instinctual shackles, although his studies of the Sioux and the Yurok ended where Roheim's work did. In 1962 Stephens[12] went back to fragmenting dozens of cultures into hundreds of pieces for the sake of a quantitative documentation of the universality of the Oedipus complex.

The need for a procedural change can be illustrated by a reference to modern human genetics and its relation to psychiatric research. Identical twins who may have reached the age of 60 are sometimes presented in order to demonstrate that the results of Rorschach and other psychological tests are similar despite different life histories. One may be married and have children, while the other stays at home with his mother, etc. The discussion can with equal validity be focused on intrapair similarities or differences. In the early days when the genetic aspects of human behavior had still to be validated, it was necessary, of course, to place the emphasis on possible similarities. With the importance of psychiatric genetics fully established, this kind of emphasis is no longer needed. Today we are more aware of the opportunity that two individuals with similar biological equipment provide for studying what accounts for the differences in their lives.*

---

* Kallmann's [13] genetic studies of suicide in twins have ruled out the possibility of a special genetic factor predisposing a person to commit suicide.

In the area of psychosocial studies more can be learned from appraising the extent to which social institutions influence unconscious psychodynamic constellations such as the Oedipus complex than from demonstrating again and again that the Oedipus complex as a whole or in part does exist in a certain culture. Here it is most evident that one needs a frame of reference encompassing the individual's biological drives and genetic equipment, the psychosocial attitudes of his culture and his psychodynamic integration of both sets of factors.

✿   ✿   ✿

Separate issues are presented by those questions that cross-cultural research does not deal with or can only speculate about. One such question was raised by a young Swedish colleague who had read an account of this study in a psychiatric journal: "What you say about Swedes is interesting and seems true, but you don't answer the really important question of why Johanson is suicidal and Carlson is not."

How valid is this objection? We speak of the tubercle bacillus as the cause of tuberculosis and make every effort toward its extinction in order to cure the patient. Yet of two people who have equal exposure to the infectious agent only one may actually develop the disease. The use of the concept of varying resistance as an explanation merely serves to emphasize that almost all pathological conditions have a multiplicity of causative factors. To employ a somewhat closer medical analogy— if cigarette smoking is established as a causative factor in lung cancer, will the issue really be why only Johanson succumbed to lung cancer although Carlson as well as he smoked two packs a day?

Another obvious inquiry would be that into the origin of differences in social institutions. Why do the Danes do things one way, the Swedes another, and the Norwegians still another? In primitive societies such comparisons are facilitated by the fact that problems of adaptation tend to vary more from culture to culture. In modern societies both adaptive problems and the techniques for dealing with them seem to be, at least on the surface, more similar.

One might speculate, for example, about the reason why Norwegian children are given more physical freedom than Danish children. By tradition the Norwegians have been fishing people and the boys had to be out in the boats with their fathers from an early age. Perhaps both mother and son had to be prepared for this separation as a necessity of life dictated by society. How about the early separation of mother and child in Sweden? Did it possibly originate in different farm duties required of Swedish and Danish women? Such questions cannot be adequately answered without the research of a social historian.

Whenever psychosocial studies are aimed at exploring specific questions, varying from the psychological consequences of particular social institutions to such clinical or social problems as crime, suicide, neurosis, etc., they are on familiar ground. However, if they are used to form judgments about the internal or foreign policies of a nation, the footing is less solid.

This limitation must be kept in mind with respect to the one area in the recent political history of Scandinavia where such questions are frequently encountered, i.e., the different roles played by the three Scandinavian countries during the war.

William Shirer[14] emphasized the difference between the Danish and Norwegian reactions to the German attack and occupation. Considering military resistance as futile, the Danes yielded to the German ultimatum "under protest" and were regarded by the Germans as a "model protectorate" for the first few years of the occupation. Since neither the government nor the civilian population caused much trouble, the occupying forces tended to be lenient toward the Danes as a whole, and even the Danish Jews remained relatively unmolested until 1943. The Norwegians rejected the German ultimatum and fought stubbornly for several months. Norwegian Home Front resistance was both military and civilian in nature and became a well organized operation long before allied success could be foreseen. The Norwegians paid heavily for their resistance, and extermination of the Norwegian Jews was only a part of it.

Of course there were some exceptions, and Henrik Kauffman in Denmark and Vidkun Quisling in Norway were merely the best known. Resistance gradually developed in Denmark too, particularly from 1943 on. Partly because of this increasing resistance, the Germans decided in 1943 to liquidate the 8,000

Danish Jews, whereupon the Danes hid them or helped them escape to Sweden and thus exposed themselves to the fury of the German retaliation.

Shirer described Sweden's "un-neutral concessions" to Germany, particularly in supplying the Germans with war materials and in transporting German troops through Sweden to Norway. Of course, it was the Swedish government that adhered to the policy of insuring neutrality at all cost. Apparently, however, the policy was supported by a majority of the population. The fluctuations in Swedish policy with the turning tides of the war were also reported by Shirer.

The situational circumstances were different in each of the three countries. Norway's mountainous terrain aided and encouraged resistance; Denmark's flatness precluded effective defense as well as the possibility of English military aid, which was helpful in Norway for a while. Certainly Norway wanted as eagerly as Sweden to be neutral, and the choice of invading the former country was made by Germany on the basis of her own geopolitical considerations rather than the wishes of Norwegians or Swedes. Pointing to the hopelessness of the Swedish position in 1940, Shirer quoted the Swedish reply to a Norwegian note of protest: "All neutrality policy has its limits in the possibilities open to the neutral state." It is also clear that in terms of her ability to help Norway and Denmark, a neutral Sweden was more useful than an occupied Sweden. The Swedes were extremely generous in sending food, clothing, medical supplies, and money for relief. By the end of the war Sweden had spent three quarters of a billion dollars in relief and had sheltered several hundred thousand European refugees. "No people in Europe was more generous than the Swedes."

Despite these considerations, Shirer was critical of the Swedish and Danish policies; his admiration for Scandinavian social democracy was tempered by his disapproval of the roles which these two countries played in the first war years. Shirer has been the conscience of more than Scandinavia as far as World War II is concerned, and it would not be appropriate here to discuss the morality or even the wisdom of the policies followed by the Scandinavian countries during that period.

One may ask, however, whether there might have been a relation between certain character traits of the individual Dane (difficulty in mobilizing aggression and a tendency to passivity) and the role accepted by the population during the first years of the German occupation. Also, was the different reaction in Norway related to the individual Norwegian's ability to respond with and sustain anger? Furthermore, was Sweden's neutrality in any way a reflection of the tendency of her citizens to handle aggression by detachment and withdrawal?

Although these parallels are suggestive, they are only parallels. Inasmuch as the author came to the Scandinavian countries 15 years after the war, he can merely raise such questions but not really answer them.

The task of predicting future suicide trends in Scandinavia is equally hazardous. For example, the social welfare measures instituted by Sweden and Denmark do not yet seem to have been followed by a significant change in the character of these people. Apparently Danish passivity antedated these measures and Swedish competitiveness was more influenced by her industrialization.

Denmark and Norway have long been the poor relations of wealthy Sweden. Hence it may have been advisable for them to control aspirations and competitiveness as long as the potential values of initiative and ambition were limited. If Denmark and Norway continue to prosper with western Europe, it is conceivable that growing prosperity will gradually change their attitudes toward aspiration and success. In the case of Denmark a shift away from dependent character attitudes would be likely to reduce the "dependency loss" suicides still so prevalent there. In Norway's case an increase in opportunities and national wealth could stimulate the people's aspirations and might indirectly result, as it has elsewhere, in a higher suicide rate.

The Swedish situation seems to be the most difficult. There is reason for assuming that aspirations in Sweden will continue to grow at a similar rate to that of the rest of the Western world. As long as there is a tendency toward an early mother-child separation, with its deleterious effects on the development of affectivity, and as long as general performance expectations remain high, the Swedish suicide rate might increase still further. Of course, the speculative nature of such statements needs no particular emphasis.

*   *   *

It is not the aim of this study to establish or grade the superiority of one society over another, and even if it were, it could not be done. The main objective is to study the consequences of differing social institutions. Needless to say, such work is apt to arouse some defensiveness and will feed certain prejudices. If it did not, it would probably have failed to uncover significant facts. Although the Danes have been accustomed to speaking humorously about their high suicide rate, they are somewhat oversensitive to any attention given to it by a foreigner. The author had several opportunities to talk to Danish colleagues about this study. On two occasions he was interrupted at once with the non-sequitur "What about homicide in the United States?" In subsequent lectures it was mentioned immediately that the homicide figures were comparatively high in the United States and low in Denmark. With this assurance that their country was not about to be criticized, the group was willing to listen to the actual report with relaxed attention.

However, the tendency to feel hurt or unfairly criticized by a psychosocial analysis is not peculiar to the Danes. In an analysis of any majority or minority group in the United States, one would encounter some people who are sure of having been attacked, and some—either within or outside the group—who would use any findings to support their own prejudices.

Social institutions cannot and should not be changed lightly. It is much easier to learn the effect of certain institutions than to foresee the consequences change might bring. Our present knowledge is insufficient for engaging in psychosocial engineering with much confidence.

Since the ways in which a society does things are likely to have advantages as well as a price to be paid, we need inquiries into the consequences of social institutions to tell us something about how much we are paying for following a given procedure. Cross-cultural studies can help us evaluate the alternatives intelligently. And in such studies, psychodynamics, properly utilized, serves as a sensitive instrument.

Notes and References

Chapter I. The Problem

1. Edward Sapir's discussion of Russian national character in "Culture, Genuine and Spurious," *American Journal of Sociology*, 29:401-429, Boston, 1934, were forerunners of the interest in national character in 1924, and Ruth Benedict's *Patterns of Culture*, Houghton Mifflin, the 1940's reflected in such works as Margaret Mead's *And Keep Your Powder Dry*, William Morrow, New York, 1943, and Geoffry Gorer's *The American People*, W.W. Norton & Co., 1948.
2. Abram Kardiner
    The Individual and His Society, Columbia University Press, 1939.
    The Psychological Frontiers of Society, Columbia University Press, 1945.
3. David Rodnick
    The Norwegians, Public Affairs Press, 1955.
4. Herbert Hendin, Willard Gaylin, and Arthur Carr
    "Psychoanalytic Interviewing with Non-Patients" (not yet published).
5. It would be too lengthy to list individually the well over a hundred statistical bulletins used as sources of information. Anyone wishing to obtain all the relevant statistical data can readily do so from the following five major sources:
    1. The Statistical Section of the Danish National Health Service in Copenhagen.
    2. The Swedish Central Bureau of Statistics in Stockholm.
    3. The Norwegian Central Bureau of Statistics in Oslo.
    4. The National Vital Statistics Division of the Department of Health, Education & Welfare in Washington.
    5. *The Epidemiological & Vital Statistics Reports* of the World Health Organization in Geneva. (Vol. 9, No. 4, 1956, in particular contains an excellent summary of international suicide statistics in the first half of this century.)
    Almost all the Scandinavian bulletins, and their statistical yearbooks in particular, contain English captions and can be used by the English reader not versed in any of the Scandinavian languages.
6. A clear picture of the comparative European suicide rates and trends in this century can be found in Karen Dreyer's article, "Comparative Suicide Statistics," *Danish Medical Bulletin*, Vol. 6, No. 3, pp. 65-81, May 1959.
7. Dalgaard's point that in Denmark a doctor trained in forensic medicine sees "unnatural deaths," while in Norway only an ordinary physician does so, is not significant in terms of any possible effect on the respec-

tive suicide figures in the two countries. See Jørgen Dalgaard, "Om International Sammenligning af Selvmordfrekvenser. Nogle Kritiske Betragtninger" (Critical Remarks on the International Comparison of Suicidal Rates), *Sociologiske Meddelelser,* Vol. 1, No. 7, pp. 53-60, 1962.

Chapter II. Durkheim and Freud

1. Emile Durkheim
   Division of Labor in Society (1893), The Free Press, Glencoe, Ill., 1933.
   The Rules of Sociological Method (1894), The Free Press, Glencoe, Ill., 1938.
   Suicide (1897), The Free Press, Glencoe, Ill., 1951.
   This chapter deals with Durkheim in reference to the problem of suicide, and it is not relevant to this purpose to deal with Durkheim's more important role as one of the founders of modern sociology. A comprehensive evaluation of Durkheim's work and methodology is contained in Harry Alpert's *Emile Durkheim and His Sociology* (Columbia University Press, 1939), Russell & Russell, New York, 1961.

2. Two of the best known of such studies are Ruth Cavan's *Suicide,* The University of Chicago Press, 1928, and Dublin's and Bunzel's *To Be or Not To Be: A Study of Suicide,* Random House, New York, 1933.

3. Sigmund Freud
   "Psychogenesis of a Case of Homosexuality in a Woman" (1920). *Collected Papers,* Vol. II, pp. 202-231, Hogarth Press, London, 1949.

4. Sigmund Freud
   "Mourning and Melancholia" (1916). *Collected Papers.* Vol. IV, pp. 152-170, Hogarth Press, London, 1949.

5. Sigmund Freud
   Civilization and its Discontents (1930), Hogarth Press, London, 1949.

6. Sigmund Freud
   Beyond the Pleasure Principle (1920), Hogarth Press, London, 1948.

7. John Dewey
   Human Nature and Conduct (1922), Modern Library, New York, 1930.

8. Gregory Zilboorg
   "Considerations on Suicide with particular reference to that of the young." *Amer. J. of Orthopsychiatry,* 7:15-31, 1937.

9. Karl Menninger
   Man Against Himself, Harcourt Brace, New York, 1938.

10. Sigmund Freud
    Totem and Taboo (1913), Modern Library, New York, 1938.

11. Gregory Zilboorg
    "Suicide among Civilized and Primitive Races." *Amer. J. of Psychiat.,* 92:1347-1369, 1936.

Chapter III. The Psychodynamics of Suicide

1. Sandor Rado
   "The Problem of Melancholia" (1927). *Collected Papers*, Vol. I, pp. 47-63, Grune & Stratton, New York, 1956.
   "Psychodynamics of Depression from the Etiological Point of View" (1951). *Collected Papers*, Vol. I, pp. 235-242, Grune & Stratton, New York, 1956.
   "Hedonic Control, Action-Self, and the Depressive Spell" (1954, Revised 1955). *Collected Papers*, Vol. I, pp. 286-311, Grune & Stratton, New York, 1956.
   "The Automatic Motivating System of Depressive Behavior" (1961). *Collected Papers*, Vol. II, pp. 163-177, Grune & Stratton, New York, 1962.

2. Herbert Hendin
   "Attempted Suicide: A Psychiatric and Statistical Study." *Psychiat. Quart.*, 24:39-46, 1950.

3. Farberow and Schneidman
   "Suicide and Death," a chapter in the book *The Meaning of Death*, edited by Herman Feifel, McGraw-Hill, New York, 1959.

4. E. Stengel
   "Recent Research into Suicide and Attempted Suicide," *The Amer. J. of Psychiat.*, Vol. 118:725-727, 1962.

5. Ruth Ettlinger of Södersjukhuset, Stockholm, in a personal communication. See also Ruth Ettlinger and Per Flordh, "Attempted Suicide: Experience of Five Hundred Cases at a General Hospital." *Acta Psychiatrica et Neurologica Scandinavica*, Supplement 103, pp. 4-45, Copenhagen, 1955.

6. Karl Menninger
   Man Against Himself, Harcourt Brace, New York, 1938.

7. Sigmund Freud
   "Thoughts for the Times on War and Death" (1915). *Collected Papers*, Vol. IV, pp. 288-317, Hogarth Press, London, 1949.

8. Gregory Zilboorg
   "Suicide among Civilized and Primitive Races." *Amer. J. of Psychiat.*, 92:1347-1369, 1936.
   "The Sense of Immortality." *Psychoan. Quart.*, 7:171-199, 1938.

9. Herman Feifel makes a similar point in his article, "Attitudes toward Death in Some Mentally Ill Populations," contained in *The Meaning of Death*, edited by Feifel, McGraw-Hill, 1959. While the book contains articles about death and a chapter on suicide (see footnote 3), it does not contain any study devoted to the meanings of death for suicidal patients.

10. Herbert Hendin
    "Suicide." *Psychiat. Quart.*, 30:267-282, 1956.
    "Suicide in Denmark." *Psychiat. Quart.*, 34:443-460, 1960.
    "Suicide: Psychoanalytic Point of View." In *The Cry for Help*,

edited by Farberow & Schneidman, pp. 181-192, McGraw-Hill, New York, 1961.

"Suicide in Sweden." *Psychiat. Quart.*, 35:1-28, 1962.

"The Psychodynamics of Suicide." *The J. of Nervous and Mental Disease*, 136:236-244, 1963.

Chapter IV. Suicide in Denmark

1. Kirsten Rudfeld
   "Suicide in Denmark—1956," *Acta Sociologica*, Vol. VI, No. 3, pp. 203-214, Copenhagen, 1962.
2. Grethe Pærregaard
   Selvmordforsøg og Selvmord i København (Attempted Suicide and Suicide in Copenhagen), presented as a doctoral thesis in October, 1962, printed in 1963 by Aarhuus Stiftsbogtrykkerie.
3. *Tales of Grimm and Andersen*, Modern Library, New York, 1952.
4. For a good account of the Danish social welfare measures, see *Social Denmark*, Socialt Tidskrift, Copenhagen, 1947.
5. For a comparison of the social welfare measures in the Scandinavian countries, see *Freedom and Welfare: Social Patterns in the Northern Countries of Europe,* sponsored by the Ministries of Social Affairs of Denmark, Finland, Iceland, Norway and Sweden, 1953.

Chapter V. Suicide in Sweden

1. All of the novels and stories specifically referred to in the discussion of Pär Lagerkvist are available in English: *The Dwarf,* Hill and Wang, 1945; *Barabbas,* Random House, 1951; *The Eternal Smile and Other Stories,* Random House, 1954. Lagerkvist's collected poems, which in a few lines convey the same feeling as his novels, have not been translated into English.
2. The English reader can get a feeling for the Swedish preoccupation with death from reading both Stig Dagerman's *A Burnt Child,* William Morrow & Co. and *The Games of Night,* The Bodley Head, London, 1959. See also Per Hallström's *Selected Short Stories,* published by The American-Scandinavian Foundation, New York, 1922.
3. For a good one-volume survey of the Swedish social welfare programs, see *Social Sweden,* published by The Swedish Social Welfare Board, Gernandt's Book Co., Stockholm, 1952.
4. Eli F. Hecksher's work, condensed into a one-volume English edition, gives a good picture of the remarkable transformation of Sweden from

an economically backward country to one of the most advanced countries in Europe. *An Economic History of Sweden,* Harvard University Press, Cambridge, 1954.

5. An excellent survey of Swedish literature is Alrik Gustafson's *A History of Swedish Literature,* published for The American-Scandinavian Foundation by the University of Minnesota Press, Minneapolis, 1961.

6. For a picture of the development of economic and political democracy in Sweden, Norway and Denmark, see *Scandinavian Democracy,* published jointly by The Danish Institute, The Swedish Institute and The Norwegian Office of Cultural Relations together with The American-Scandinavian Foundation, Copenhagen, 1958.

7. Eva Moberg
   Kvinnor och Människor (Women and Society), Albert Bonniers Förlag, Stockholm, 1962.

Chapter VI. Suicide in Norway

1. Gregory Zilboorg
   "Differential Diagnostic Types of Suicide." *Archives of Neurology and Psychiatry,* 35:270-291, 1936.
   "Considerations on Suicide with Particular Reference to that of the Young." American Journal of Orthopsychiatry, 7:15-31, 1937.

2. Nic Waal
   Er Det Foreldrenes Skyld? (Are The Parents Guilty?) J. W. Cappelen Co., Oslo, 1962. The book appeared first in Swedish in 1954 under the title *Det Finns Inga Stygga Föräldrar* (There Are No Bad Parents), Wahlstrom and Wildstrand, Stockholm, 1959, and has also appared in Danish; however, there is no English edition.

3. Sigurd Hoel
   A Day in October, Coward McCann, New York, 1932.

4. Asbjørnsen and Moe
   Samlede Eventyr (Collected Tales), Gyldendal Norsk Forlag, Oslo, 1940. A fair selection of the tales is available in English in *Norway's Folk Tales,* published by Dreyers Forlag, Oslo, 1960.

5. David Rodnick
   The Norwegians, Public Affairs Press, 1955, Washington, D.C.

6. Thomas D. Eliot and Arthur Hillman
   Norway's Families, University of Pennsylvania Press, 1960.

7. For a good description of the first two years of the German occupation of Norway and of Norwegian home front resistance see *They Came as Friends,* Tor Myklebost, Country Life Press, Garden City, New York, 1943. A comparison of the role of all three Scandinavian countries during the war may be found in William Shirer's *The Challenge of Scandinavia,* Little, Brown & Co., Boston, 1955.

8. All of the Ibsen plays referred to are also available in many different English editions, which need not be specifically enumerated. A good

background survey of Norwegian literature including Ibsen and Asbjørnsen and Moe is Harald Beyer's *A History of Norwegian Literature*, published by the New York University Press for The American-Scandinavian Foundation in 1956.

9. E. Schiødt
    Contribution to the "Round Table Conference on the Incidences and Causes of Suicide," *Acta Psychiatrica et Neurologica Scandinavica* Supplement, 136:433-434, 1959. Contribution to the panel on *Suicidalhyppighed og Årsagsforhold* (Frequency and Causes of Suicide), *Nord. Med.* 63:624, 1960.

Chapter VII.   Conclusions and Applications

1. Karl Gustav Dahlgren's *On Suicide and Attempted Suicide*, Lindstedt, Lund, 1945, can be recommended to the reader interested in the Scandinavian psychiatric approach to the study of suicide. Dahlgren's monograph set the pattern for a good deal of the subsequent work in Scandinavia and was also the first published account of a follow-up study on a large group of attempted suicides.

2. Kinsey, Pomeroy, Martin
    Sexual Behavior in the Human Male, W. B. Saunders Co., Philadelphia and London, 1948.

3. Sigmund Freud
    Totem and Taboo (1913), Modern Library, New York, 1938.

4. Geza Roheim was a prolific writer with approximately 200 articles and books to his credit. *The Origin and Function of Culture*, Nervous and Mental Disease Monograph, No. 69, New York, 1943, and *Psychoanalysis and Anthropology: Culture, Personality, and the Unconscious*, International Universities Press, New York, 1950, provide a representative sample of his approach to psychoanalytic anthropology.

5. Abram Kardiner
    The Individual and His Society, Columbia University Press, New York, 1939.

6. Clyde Kluckhohn's debt to Roheim and to classical psychoanalytic theory is both implicitly and explicitly stated in his last book, *Culture and Behavior*, The Free Press, Glencoe, Ill., 1962. Margaret Mead in *Male and Female*, Morrow, 1948, New York, specifically acknowledges her debt to Roheim.

7. Erich Fromm
    Escape From Freedom, Rinehart & Co., New York, 1941.
    Man For Himself, Rinehart & Co., New York, 1947.
    The Sane Society, Rinehart & Co., New York, 1955.

8. For a full critique of Fromm's work and a comparative discussion of Freud, Fromm and Kardiner and their contributions to a science of society, see Martin Birnbach's *Neo-Freudian Social Philosophy*, Stanford University Press, Stanford, 1961.

9. Abram Kardiner
   The Individual and His Society, Columbia University Press, 1939.
   The Psychological Frontiers of Society, Columbia University Press, 1945.
   Abram Kardiner and Edward Preble
   They Studied Man, The World Publishing Co., Cleveland, 1961.
10. Abram Kardiner and Lionel Ovesey
   The Mark of Oppression: A Psychosocial Study of the American Negro, W. W. Norton & Co., New York, 1951.
11. Erik Erikson
   Childhood and Society, W. W. Norton & Co., New York, 1950.
12. William N. Stephens
   The Oedipus Complex: Cross-Cultural Evidence, The Free Press, Glencoe, Ill., 1962.
13. Franz J. Kallmann and Mary M. Anastasio
   "Twin Studies on the Psychopathology of Suicide." *J. of Nervous and Mental Disease,* 105:40-55, 1947.
   Franz J. Kallmann, Joseph De Porte, Elizabeth De Porte and Lissy Feingold
   "Suicide in Twins and Only Children." *Amer. J. of Genetics.*" 1:113-126, 1949.
14. William L. Shirer
   The Challenge of Scandinavia, Little, Brown & Co., Boston, 1955.
   The Rise and Fall of The Third Reich, Simon & Schuster, New York, 1960.

Name Index

Subject Index